GRC in Cybersecurity: Complete Guide

James Relington

DEDICATION

This book is dedicated to all the professionals working tirelessly to secure digital identities and protect organizations from ever-evolving threats. To the cybersecurity teams, IT administrators, and identity management experts who ensure safe and seamless access for users— your work is invaluable. And to my family and friends, whose support and encouragement made this journey possible, thank you.

AKNOWLEDGEMENTS

I would like to express my deepest gratitude to everyone who contributed to the creation of this book. To my colleagues and mentors in the cybersecurity and identity management field, your insights and expertise have been invaluable. To the organizations and professionals who shared their experiences and best practices, your contributions have enriched this work. A special thank you to my family and friends for their unwavering support and encouragement throughout this journey. Finally, to the readers, thank you for your interest in identity lifecycle management—may this book help you navigate the evolving landscape of digital security with confidence.

Introduction to GRC in Cybersecurity

Governance, Risk, and Compliance (GRC) has become an essential framework in the field of cybersecurity, helping organizations navigate complex regulatory environments, mitigate risks, and ensure the integrity of their security programs. In an era where cyber threats are more sophisticated than ever, businesses must implement structured policies and practices to manage security risks effectively. GRC provides a systematic approach to achieving cybersecurity objectives while aligning security initiatives with business goals, regulatory requirements, and industry standards.

Governance in cybersecurity refers to the policies, processes, and frameworks that define how security is managed within an organization. It establishes accountability, decision-making structures, and strategic alignment between cybersecurity efforts and business objectives. Effective governance ensures that security leaders, executives, and stakeholders understand their roles and responsibilities in protecting digital assets. Without proper governance, cybersecurity programs often lack direction, leading to fragmented security practices, inefficient resource allocation, and vulnerabilities that attackers can exploit. Organizations must develop clear cybersecurity policies, enforce compliance with internal controls, and continuously assess the effectiveness of their governance models.

Risk management in cybersecurity focuses on identifying, analyzing, and mitigating potential threats to an organization's information systems. Every business faces risks from cyber threats, including malware attacks, data breaches, insider threats, and vulnerabilities in software and hardware. A strong risk management approach involves assessing the likelihood and impact of security incidents, implementing controls to reduce exposure, and continuously monitoring the evolving threat landscape. Cyber risk assessments help organizations prioritize security investments, ensuring that resources are allocated efficiently to mitigate the most critical risks. The ability to quantify risk allows organizations to make informed decisions and balance security efforts with business needs.

Compliance plays a critical role in cybersecurity by ensuring that organizations adhere to legal, regulatory, and industry-specific requirements. Governments and regulatory bodies have introduced stringent cybersecurity laws to protect sensitive information, safeguard consumer data, and maintain the integrity of digital systems. Compliance frameworks such as the General Data Protection Regulation (GDPR), the Payment Card Industry Data Security Standard (PCI DSS), and the National Institute of Standards and Technology (NIST) Cybersecurity Framework provide guidelines for organizations to follow. Failure to comply with these regulations can result in severe financial penalties, reputational damage, and legal consequences. Implementing a robust compliance program not only helps organizations avoid regulatory fines but also enhances trust with customers, partners, and stakeholders.

The integration of GRC into cybersecurity enables organizations to build resilient security programs that address governance challenges, manage risks proactively, and meet compliance obligations. A well-structured GRC approach fosters a culture of security awareness and accountability, ensuring that cybersecurity is not merely an IT concern but a core component of business strategy. Organizations that fail to integrate GRC into their cybersecurity efforts often struggle with inconsistencies in security policies, poor risk visibility, and difficulties in responding to regulatory changes. By establishing a unified GRC framework, businesses can streamline security processes, improve decision-making, and enhance their ability to respond to cyber threats effectively.

One of the key challenges in implementing GRC in cybersecurity is the dynamic nature of cyber risks. Attackers continuously develop new techniques to exploit vulnerabilities, making it essential for organizations to adapt their security strategies in real time. Traditional security models that rely solely on compliance checklists are no longer sufficient in addressing modern cyber threats. Instead, organizations must adopt a risk-based approach that focuses on continuous monitoring, threat intelligence, and adaptive security measures. This approach ensures that cybersecurity efforts remain relevant and effective against evolving threats.

Another significant challenge is achieving alignment between cybersecurity and business objectives. Many organizations struggle with the misconception that cybersecurity is solely a technical function rather than a strategic business enabler. Effective GRC implementation requires collaboration between IT teams, executive leadership, legal departments, and compliance officers. Security leaders must communicate the value of cybersecurity in business terms, demonstrating how security investments contribute to risk reduction, regulatory compliance, and long-term business success. When cybersecurity is aligned with business goals, organizations can achieve a balance between security and operational efficiency.

Technology plays a crucial role in supporting GRC initiatives in cybersecurity. Organizations increasingly leverage automation, artificial intelligence, and machine learning to enhance risk management, streamline compliance efforts, and improve governance practices. GRC platforms provide centralized dashboards that enable real-time risk monitoring, policy enforcement, and compliance tracking. These technologies help organizations reduce manual processes, minimize human error, and improve the overall efficiency of their security programs. However, while technology can enhance GRC capabilities, it is essential to remember that successful implementation also requires strong leadership, clear policies, and a culture of security awareness.

An effective GRC strategy in cybersecurity is not a one-time effort but a continuous process of evaluation and improvement. Organizations must regularly assess their governance frameworks, update risk management practices, and stay informed about regulatory changes. Security leaders should conduct regular audits, penetration testing, and incident response exercises to identify weaknesses and enhance their security posture. Additionally, employee training and awareness programs are vital in ensuring that all personnel understand their role in maintaining cybersecurity compliance and mitigating risks. A proactive approach to GRC enables organizations to stay ahead of threats, respond to incidents more effectively, and build a resilient security posture that supports long-term business growth.

As cybersecurity threats become increasingly sophisticated, the importance of GRC continues to grow. Organizations that embrace GRC principles are better equipped to navigate regulatory complexities, manage cyber risks effectively, and strengthen their overall security framework. By integrating governance, risk management, and compliance into their cybersecurity strategy, businesses can create a structured and resilient security environment that not only protects digital assets but also enhances trust and credibility in an interconnected world.

The Evolution of Cybersecurity Governance

The concept of cybersecurity governance has undergone significant transformation over the years, evolving from a fragmented set of security policies to a structured and strategic discipline that aligns security with business objectives. As organizations have become more reliant on digital technologies, the need for a comprehensive governance framework to manage cyber risks, regulatory requirements, and security investments has grown exponentially. Cybersecurity governance today is no longer just about protecting systems from external threats; it is about embedding security into the corporate structure, ensuring accountability, and fostering a culture of continuous risk management.

In the early days of computing, cybersecurity governance was a minimal concern. Organizations focused primarily on physical security, controlling access to mainframe computers housed in secured environments. Security policies, if they existed, were basic and primarily designed to ensure that only authorized personnel could access computing resources. The idea of cyber threats was virtually nonexistent, as networks were closed, and the risk of unauthorized access was relatively low. During this period, governance was informal, and security responsibilities often fell on IT personnel without formalized oversight from executive leadership.

The rise of networked systems and the internet in the late 20th century brought new challenges that forced organizations to rethink their approach to security governance. As businesses interconnected their systems, they became vulnerable to remote attacks, data breaches, and unauthorized access. The need for structured security policies became evident, leading to the creation of access controls, password policies, and basic security protocols. However, governance was still primarily reactive, focusing on addressing threats as they emerged rather than proactively managing security risks. Organizations struggled with inconsistent security practices, as different departments implemented their own controls without centralized oversight.

With the explosion of e-commerce, online banking, and digital transactions in the early 2000s, cybersecurity governance took a more formalized shape. Regulatory bodies and industry groups began introducing security standards and compliance frameworks to address the growing risks of cybercrime and data breaches. The development of regulations such as the Sarbanes-Oxley Act (SOX) in the United States and the ISO 27001 standard for information security management systems (ISMS) marked the beginning of a governance-driven approach to cybersecurity. Organizations were required to implement security controls, document policies, and establish accountability for data protection. Governance was no longer an afterthought but a business requirement, driven by regulatory compliance and the need to protect sensitive information.

The rise of sophisticated cyber threats, including malware, phishing, and advanced persistent threats (APTs), further shaped cybersecurity governance in the 2010s. Organizations recognized that compliance alone was not enough to safeguard against evolving cyber risks. A shift towards risk-based governance began to emerge, emphasizing the need for continuous risk assessments, proactive security measures, and integration of cybersecurity into enterprise risk management (ERM) programs. Governance models evolved to incorporate executive oversight, with chief information security officers (CISOs) playing a critical role in defining security strategies and ensuring alignment with business objectives. Board-level discussions on cybersecurity governance became more common, as organizations faced increased pressure from regulators, customers, and investors to demonstrate their commitment to cybersecurity.

The introduction of global data protection regulations, such as the General Data Protection Regulation (GDPR) in 2018, accelerated the evolution of cybersecurity governance. Organizations were now required to implement strict data protection measures, appoint data protection officers (DPOs), and establish processes for responding to security incidents. Governance frameworks expanded to include privacy considerations, ensuring that security measures were designed not only to protect systems but also to safeguard personal data. The growing adoption of cloud computing, mobile devices, and remote work further complicated governance challenges, as organizations had to extend security controls beyond traditional corporate boundaries. Cybersecurity governance had to adapt to a decentralized environment, requiring continuous monitoring, third-party risk management, and automated compliance solutions.

Today, cybersecurity governance is a fundamental aspect of corporate strategy, integrating security, risk management, and compliance into a unified framework. Organizations recognize that cybersecurity is not just a technical issue but a business imperative that requires leadership, investment, and cross-functional collaboration. Governance frameworks such as the NIST Cybersecurity Framework, COBIT, and ISO 27001 provide structured approaches for managing cybersecurity risks and ensuring regulatory compliance. Organizations implement governance structures that define roles and responsibilities, establish cybersecurity committees, and develop reporting mechanisms to track security performance.

The rapid advancement of emerging technologies, such as artificial intelligence (AI), the Internet of Things (IoT), and blockchain, presents new governance challenges that organizations must address. AI-driven attacks, deepfake threats, and supply chain vulnerabilities require adaptive governance models that can evolve with technological advancements. Organizations must embrace a dynamic approach to cybersecurity governance, incorporating threat intelligence, continuous monitoring, and predictive analytics to stay ahead of emerging risks. Governance is no longer static; it must be agile, data-driven, and capable of responding to an increasingly complex cyber threat landscape.

Looking ahead, the future of cybersecurity governance will be shaped by increased regulatory scrutiny, greater reliance on automation, and the need for enhanced collaboration between governments, businesses, and industry groups. Organizations will need to invest in cybersecurity awareness programs, strengthen incident response capabilities, and adopt zero-trust security models to mitigate risks effectively. Cybersecurity governance will continue to evolve, driven by the need for resilience, transparency, and accountability in an interconnected world. Organizations that embrace governance as a strategic enabler will be better positioned to manage cyber risks, protect their digital assets, and maintain trust in an era of constant cyber threats.

Risk Management Fundamentals

Risk management is a critical component of cybersecurity, enabling organizations to identify, assess, and mitigate threats that could compromise their digital assets, operations, and overall business continuity. In a constantly evolving threat landscape, risk management provides a structured approach to evaluating potential vulnerabilities and implementing security measures to minimize damage. Organizations that fail to prioritize risk management expose themselves to financial losses, regulatory penalties, reputational damage, and operational disruptions. A well-defined risk management strategy helps organizations make informed decisions about resource allocation, security investments, and incident response planning.

At its core, risk management in cybersecurity involves three primary elements: threat identification, vulnerability assessment, and impact analysis. Threat identification focuses on recognizing potential dangers that could exploit weaknesses in an organization's infrastructure. These threats can originate from various sources, including cybercriminals, insider threats, nation-state actors, and natural disasters. Understanding the nature and intent of these threats is essential in formulating an effective defense strategy. Vulnerability assessment involves analyzing weaknesses within an organization's IT environment, including software flaws, misconfigured systems, and inadequate access controls. By identifying these weaknesses, organizations can take proactive steps to mitigate risks before attackers exploit them. Impact analysis evaluates the potential consequences of a successful cyberattack, measuring financial losses, reputational harm, regulatory non-compliance, and operational downtime.

The risk management process follows a cyclical approach, beginning with risk identification and followed by risk analysis, evaluation, treatment, and continuous monitoring. The identification phase involves gathering intelligence on potential risks by conducting security assessments, reviewing past incidents, and leveraging threat intelligence sources. Organizations must maintain an up-to-date inventory of digital assets, including hardware, software, and sensitive data, to understand what needs protection. The risk analysis phase assesses the likelihood and potential impact of each identified risk. Quantitative and qualitative risk assessment methods help organizations prioritize risks based on their severity and probability. Quantitative assessments assign numerical values to risks, estimating potential financial losses and operational impact. Qualitative assessments, on the other hand, categorize risks based on subjective judgment, using scales such as low, medium, and high.

Once risks are analyzed, the next step is evaluation, where organizations determine whether risks fall within acceptable tolerance levels or require mitigation strategies. Cybersecurity risk appetite varies between organizations, depending on industry regulations, business objectives, and risk tolerance levels. High-risk industries, such as finance and healthcare, often have lower risk tolerance due to strict compliance requirements and the potential for severe consequences following a breach. Organizations must define clear risk thresholds and develop governance structures to ensure security measures align with business priorities. Risk treatment involves implementing security controls to reduce, transfer, avoid, or accept risks. Risk reduction strategies focus on strengthening security measures, such as implementing encryption, multi-factor authentication, and intrusion detection systems. Risk transfer involves shifting liability through cybersecurity insurance policies or outsourcing security functions to third-party providers. Risk avoidance entails eliminating activities that introduce unacceptable levels of risk, such as discontinuing the use of vulnerable technologies. Risk acceptance occurs when organizations recognize a risk but choose not to take immediate action due to cost considerations or low probability of occurrence.

Continuous monitoring and reassessment are essential to maintaining an effective risk management program. Cyber threats evolve rapidly, and security controls must be regularly updated to address emerging risks. Organizations employ security information and event management (SIEM) systems, endpoint detection and response (EDR) tools, and automated compliance solutions to track security events and detect anomalies. Conducting periodic risk assessments, penetration testing, and red team exercises helps organizations identify weaknesses and refine their cybersecurity strategies. Security awareness training for employees also plays a vital role in risk management, as human error remains one of the most significant contributors to cyber incidents.

A comprehensive risk management strategy requires collaboration between multiple stakeholders, including executive leadership, IT teams, legal departments, and compliance officers. The involvement of senior management ensures that cybersecurity risk is recognized as a business priority rather than a purely technical concern. Board members and executives must be educated on cyber risks to make informed decisions regarding security investments and risk mitigation strategies. Organizations that integrate cybersecurity risk management into enterprise risk management (ERM) frameworks achieve a more holistic approach, ensuring that security is aligned with financial, operational, and reputational risks.

Regulatory compliance plays a significant role in shaping risk management practices. Laws and industry standards, such as the General Data Protection Regulation (GDPR), the NIST Cybersecurity Framework, and the Payment Card Industry Data Security Standard (PCI DSS), establish guidelines for organizations to follow in managing cyber risks. Compliance requirements mandate the implementation of security controls, regular audits, and incident response procedures. However, compliance alone does not guarantee security, as cyber threats continually evolve beyond regulatory requirements. Organizations must adopt a risk-based approach that extends beyond compliance checklists and focuses on proactive threat mitigation.

Emerging technologies introduce both new opportunities and challenges in risk management. The increasing adoption of artificial intelligence (AI) and machine learning enables organizations to automate threat detection, analyze security logs, and predict cyber threats with greater accuracy. However, these technologies also introduce new risks, such as adversarial AI attacks and data privacy concerns. The Internet of Things (IoT) expands the attack surface, as connected devices often lack robust security protections. Cloud computing and remote work environments require organizations to implement zero-trust security models, ensuring that access is continuously verified and monitored. As technology advances, risk management strategies must evolve to address new attack vectors and security challenges.

Organizations that adopt a proactive and adaptive risk management approach are better equipped to withstand cyber threats and maintain business resilience. Cybersecurity is not a one-time implementation but an ongoing effort that requires vigilance, collaboration, and strategic planning. By prioritizing risk management, businesses can reduce vulnerabilities, protect sensitive data, and build trust with customers, partners, and stakeholders in an increasingly digital world.

Compliance Frameworks and Standards

Compliance frameworks and standards play a fundamental role in cybersecurity, providing organizations with structured guidelines to manage risks, protect sensitive data, and ensure adherence to legal and regulatory requirements. As cyber threats continue to evolve, businesses must adopt well-defined security controls to safeguard their digital assets while demonstrating accountability to customers, regulators, and stakeholders. Compliance is not just a legal obligation but a strategic necessity that helps organizations maintain operational resilience, avoid financial penalties, and build trust in the digital ecosystem.

The purpose of compliance frameworks is to establish a standardized approach to security and risk management. These frameworks outline best practices, control measures, and governance structures that organizations must implement to mitigate cybersecurity risks effectively. They are often designed to address specific industries, regulatory requirements, or security concerns. Compliance frameworks provide a common language for organizations, regulators, and auditors, ensuring consistency in security implementations across different sectors and geographical regions. They help businesses align their cybersecurity efforts with industry-recognized standards, reducing the likelihood of security breaches and regulatory violations.

One of the most widely recognized compliance frameworks in cybersecurity is the National Institute of Standards and Technology (NIST) Cybersecurity Framework. Developed by the U.S. government, the NIST framework provides a flexible and risk-based approach to managing cybersecurity threats. It consists of five core functions: Identify, Protect, Detect, Respond, and Recover. These functions help organizations establish a comprehensive security posture by identifying assets, implementing protective measures, monitoring for threats, responding to incidents, and ensuring business continuity. The NIST framework is widely adopted across industries due to its adaptability and alignment with global security standards.

Another critical compliance standard is the ISO/IEC 27001, an international standard for information security management systems (ISMS). This standard provides a systematic approach to securing information assets by implementing a risk-based security management system. Organizations that achieve ISO 27001 certification demonstrate their commitment to information security through the establishment of policies, procedures, and controls that protect sensitive data. The certification process involves rigorous audits, requiring organizations to document their security processes, conduct risk assessments, and continuously improve their security posture. ISO 27001 is recognized globally and is particularly valuable for organizations that operate in multiple countries or handle sensitive customer data.

In the financial sector, the Payment Card Industry Data Security Standard (PCI DSS) sets strict security requirements for businesses that process credit card transactions. PCI DSS was developed to prevent payment fraud by enforcing security controls such as encryption, secure authentication, and network segmentation. Organizations that fail to comply with PCI DSS can face hefty fines, reputational damage, and even the revocation of their ability to process card payments. Compliance with PCI DSS is not only a legal requirement for merchants but also a critical measure for protecting customer financial information from cybercriminals.

Data privacy regulations have become increasingly important in cybersecurity compliance, with the General Data Protection Regulation (GDPR) setting a high standard for data protection in the European Union. GDPR mandates that organizations implement stringent data privacy measures, obtain user consent for data processing, and notify authorities of data breaches within specific timeframes. Organizations that fail to comply with GDPR can face significant fines, with penalties reaching up to four percent of their global annual revenue. The regulation has influenced data protection laws worldwide, prompting organizations to adopt stronger privacy policies and transparency measures when handling personal data.

The Health Insurance Portability and Accountability Act (HIPAA) is a key compliance framework in the healthcare sector, designed to protect sensitive patient information. HIPAA establishes security and privacy requirements for healthcare providers, insurers, and business associates that handle electronic health records (EHRs). Compliance with HIPAA requires organizations to implement access controls, encryption, audit logs, and incident response plans to safeguard patient data from unauthorized access and breaches. Violations of HIPAA can result in substantial fines and legal consequences, making it essential for healthcare organizations to integrate cybersecurity measures into their operations.

For cloud service providers and organizations relying on cloud computing, the System and Organization Controls (SOC 2) framework provides a set of security and privacy criteria. Developed by the American Institute of Certified Public Accountants (AICPA), SOC 2 focuses on the security, availability, processing integrity, confidentiality, and privacy of cloud services. Achieving SOC 2 compliance demonstrates that a cloud provider has implemented robust security controls to protect customer data. Many organizations require SOC 2 compliance from their vendors before engaging in business relationships, making it a crucial certification for technology companies and software-as-a-service (SaaS) providers.

Cybersecurity compliance frameworks are not just about meeting regulatory requirements but also about implementing security best practices that strengthen an organization's overall security posture. While compliance frameworks provide structured guidelines, organizations must go beyond checklists and focus on continuous security improvements. Cyber threats evolve rapidly, and compliance should not be treated as a one-time effort but as an ongoing process that requires regular risk assessments, security updates, and employee training.

One of the challenges organizations face in achieving compliance is the complexity of managing multiple regulatory requirements simultaneously. Many businesses operate in highly regulated industries or global markets where they must comply with several overlapping standards. Organizations must develop an integrated compliance strategy that consolidates requirements from different frameworks, reducing redundancy and streamlining security operations. Automating compliance processes through governance, risk, and compliance (GRC) tools can help organizations monitor compliance status, track security controls, and generate audit reports more efficiently.

Another challenge is the misconception that compliance alone guarantees security. While adherence to compliance frameworks provides a strong foundation for cybersecurity, it does not eliminate all risks. Attackers continuously adapt their techniques, often exploiting gaps in compliance-driven security models. Organizations must adopt a risk-based approach that prioritizes threat intelligence, proactive defense mechanisms, and incident response readiness. Compliance should be viewed as a component of a broader cybersecurity strategy rather than a standalone requirement.

The future of cybersecurity compliance will be shaped by emerging technologies, evolving regulations, and increasing cyber threats. As artificial intelligence, blockchain, and quantum computing gain traction, regulatory bodies will introduce new compliance standards to address security concerns associated with these technologies. Organizations must stay ahead of regulatory changes by continuously updating their compliance programs, investing in advanced security solutions, and fostering a culture of cybersecurity awareness. Businesses that integrate compliance into their security strategies will not only mitigate risks but also enhance their reputation and competitive advantage in an increasingly digital world.

Governance in Cybersecurity Programs

Governance in cybersecurity programs provides the foundation for managing security risks, ensuring compliance, and aligning cybersecurity strategies with business objectives. A well-structured governance framework establishes accountability, defines roles and responsibilities, and ensures that cybersecurity initiatives are not isolated technical efforts but integrated into the organization's overall strategic planning. Without effective governance, cybersecurity programs often become fragmented, reactive, and unable to address the evolving threat landscape. Strong governance ensures that cybersecurity policies, risk management strategies, and compliance efforts are coordinated across all departments, creating a unified approach to protecting digital assets.

The primary objective of cybersecurity governance is to provide oversight and direction for security initiatives, ensuring that they support business goals while mitigating risks. Organizations must establish governance structures that define leadership roles, decision-making processes, and reporting mechanisms. The board of directors, executive leadership, and security teams must work together to create a cybersecurity governance model that is transparent, effective, and adaptable to changing threats. Governance frameworks should include policies that dictate how security measures are implemented, how risk is assessed, and how compliance with regulations is maintained.

One of the fundamental components of cybersecurity governance is defining clear roles and responsibilities. Organizations must appoint key security leaders, such as a Chief Information Security Officer (CISO), who is responsible for developing and executing the cybersecurity strategy. The CISO must collaborate with IT teams, legal departments, and risk management professionals to ensure that security policies align with business objectives and regulatory requirements. In addition to leadership roles, employees at all levels must understand their responsibilities in protecting sensitive information and following security protocols. Governance structures should establish cybersecurity committees or advisory boards that oversee security operations and ensure that security risks are properly communicated to executive leadership.

Cybersecurity governance requires a risk-based approach that prioritizes threats based on their potential impact on business operations. Organizations must conduct regular risk assessments to identify vulnerabilities, evaluate the likelihood of cyber incidents, and determine appropriate risk mitigation strategies. Risk management should be an ongoing process, integrating threat intelligence, security monitoring, and incident response capabilities. Governance frameworks should establish risk tolerance levels, ensuring that security investments are allocated efficiently based on the organization's unique risk profile. Without a risk-based governance model, organizations may either overspend on unnecessary security measures or leave critical vulnerabilities unaddressed.

Policies and procedures play a crucial role in cybersecurity governance by providing guidelines for implementing security controls, managing data protection, and responding to incidents. Governance frameworks must include policies for access control, data encryption, incident response, and security awareness training. These policies must be regularly reviewed and updated to reflect changes in regulatory requirements, technological advancements, and emerging threats. A strong governance structure ensures that cybersecurity policies are not just documents but actively enforced through monitoring, audits, and continuous improvement initiatives. Organizations should implement policy enforcement mechanisms, such as automated security controls and compliance tracking tools, to ensure that governance requirements are met consistently.

Compliance with cybersecurity regulations and industry standards is a key aspect of governance. Organizations must navigate a complex landscape of regulatory requirements, including GDPR, HIPAA, PCI DSS, and the NIST Cybersecurity Framework. Governance structures must ensure that compliance efforts are embedded into security operations rather than treated as standalone initiatives. Effective governance involves continuous compliance monitoring, conducting regular audits, and ensuring that security practices align with legal obligations. Failing to integrate compliance into governance can lead to regulatory penalties, reputational damage, and legal liabilities. Organizations must appoint compliance officers or dedicated teams to oversee regulatory adherence and coordinate with legal departments to interpret evolving cybersecurity laws.

Cybersecurity governance must also focus on incident response and crisis management. Organizations must establish governance structures that define how security incidents are reported, investigated, and mitigated. Incident response plans should outline roles, escalation procedures, and communication strategies to ensure a coordinated response to cyber threats. Governance frameworks should include post-incident review processes, allowing organizations to learn from security breaches and strengthen their security posture. By integrating incident response into governance models, organizations can enhance their ability to detect, respond to, and recover from cyberattacks effectively.

Security awareness and training programs are essential components of cybersecurity governance. Governance structures must ensure that employees, contractors, and third-party vendors receive ongoing cybersecurity education to reduce the risk of human error and insider threats. Training programs should cover topics such as phishing prevention, password management, and data handling best practices. Governance frameworks should mandate periodic security assessments and simulated cyberattack exercises to evaluate employee readiness and reinforce security awareness. Without a culture of cybersecurity awareness, governance efforts may be undermined by poor security practices at the user level.

Vendor risk management is another critical aspect of cybersecurity governance, as organizations increasingly rely on third-party vendors and cloud service providers. Governance structures must include policies for evaluating vendor security practices, conducting risk assessments, and ensuring that third-party partners comply with security requirements. Contracts and service-level agreements (SLAs) should include cybersecurity provisions, ensuring that vendors adhere to industry best practices and regulatory standards. Organizations must establish governance processes for monitoring vendor security performance and terminating relationships with vendors that fail to meet security expectations.

Metrics and key performance indicators (KPIs) are necessary for measuring the effectiveness of cybersecurity governance. Organizations must establish governance frameworks that include mechanisms for tracking security performance, assessing compliance levels, and identifying areas for improvement. Metrics such as incident response times, the number of security vulnerabilities detected, and employee compliance rates provide valuable insights into the effectiveness of governance strategies. Executive leadership and board members must receive regular reports on cybersecurity performance, enabling data-driven decision-making and continuous improvement of governance frameworks.

Cybersecurity governance must be adaptable to technological advancements and emerging threats. Organizations must establish governance structures that support continuous innovation, allowing security teams to integrate new technologies, such as artificial intelligence and automation, into their cybersecurity strategies. Governance models should encourage collaboration between IT teams, security researchers, and external cybersecurity experts to stay ahead of evolving threats. An agile governance approach enables organizations to respond proactively to new cybersecurity challenges while maintaining a strong security posture.

A well-structured cybersecurity governance framework ensures that security is not treated as an afterthought but as a core component of business operations. Organizations that prioritize governance can better manage risks, improve regulatory compliance, and strengthen their overall security resilience. Effective governance requires leadership commitment, cross-departmental collaboration, and continuous improvement efforts. By embedding cybersecurity governance into corporate strategies, organizations can create a security-first culture that enhances protection against cyber threats while supporting long-term business growth.

Cyber Risk Assessment Methodologies

Cyber risk assessment methodologies are essential for identifying, analyzing, and prioritizing threats that could impact an organization's digital infrastructure, sensitive data, and business operations. As cyber threats become increasingly sophisticated, organizations must implement structured risk assessment processes to evaluate vulnerabilities and determine the likelihood and impact of potential security incidents. A well-executed cyber risk assessment enables organizations to make informed decisions regarding risk mitigation, security investments, and regulatory compliance. Without a systematic approach to assessing cyber risks, organizations remain exposed to financial losses, reputational damage, and operational disruptions.

The foundation of a cyber risk assessment lies in understanding the assets that need protection. Organizations must first identify critical digital assets, including networks, databases, applications, intellectual property, and personally identifiable information (PII). Once the assets are defined, the next step involves determining the potential threats that could compromise their confidentiality, integrity, or availability. Cyber threats come in various forms, including malware, ransomware, phishing attacks, insider threats, and supply chain vulnerabilities. A thorough risk assessment methodology considers both external and internal threats, recognizing that human error, misconfigurations, and weak security practices can be as dangerous as external attackers.

Risk assessment methodologies typically follow a structured process that includes risk identification, risk analysis, risk evaluation, and risk treatment. The risk identification phase involves gathering information on vulnerabilities and attack vectors that could be exploited. Organizations rely on vulnerability scans, penetration testing, threat intelligence feeds, and security audits to identify potential weaknesses in their infrastructure. Security teams must also consider regulatory and compliance requirements when identifying risks, ensuring that their assessment covers industry-specific security obligations.

Once risks are identified, the risk analysis phase assesses the likelihood and impact of each risk. Risk likelihood refers to the probability of a threat successfully exploiting a vulnerability, while impact measures the potential damage to the organization. Organizations use both qualitative and quantitative methods to analyze risks. Qualitative risk assessments categorize risks into high, medium, or low based on expert judgment, interviews, and risk matrices. Quantitative assessments assign numerical values to risks, calculating financial losses, downtime costs, and breach probabilities. The choice of methodology depends on the organization's risk tolerance, regulatory requirements, and industry standards.

Several widely used cyber risk assessment frameworks provide structured methodologies for analyzing risks. The National Institute of Standards and Technology (NIST) Risk Management Framework (RMF) offers a comprehensive approach to risk assessment, guiding organizations through risk categorization, security control selection, and continuous monitoring. The ISO/IEC 27005 standard complements the ISO 27001 information security framework by providing detailed risk assessment guidelines. Another well-established methodology is the Factor Analysis of Information Risk (FAIR) model, which focuses on quantifying risk in financial terms, helping organizations prioritize security investments based on cost-benefit analysis.

The risk evaluation phase determines whether identified risks fall within acceptable tolerance levels. Organizations must define their risk appetite, which represents the level of risk they are willing to accept in pursuit of business objectives. Risks that exceed the defined threshold require mitigation strategies, while lower-priority risks may be monitored without immediate action. Risk evaluation involves consulting executive leadership, compliance officers, and security teams to ensure alignment between cybersecurity initiatives and business priorities.

Risk treatment involves selecting and implementing appropriate mitigation measures to reduce the likelihood or impact of identified risks. Organizations can choose from several risk treatment options, including risk mitigation, risk avoidance, risk transfer, and risk acceptance. Risk mitigation focuses on implementing security controls such as firewalls, intrusion detection systems, encryption, and access management to reduce risk exposure. Risk avoidance entails eliminating activities or processes that introduce significant security threats. Risk transfer shifts liability to third parties through cybersecurity insurance policies or outsourcing security functions to managed service providers. Risk acceptance occurs when organizations acknowledge a risk but decide not to take immediate action due to cost constraints or low probability of occurrence.

Continuous monitoring and reassessment are essential components of an effective cyber risk assessment methodology. Cyber threats constantly evolve, and security controls must be regularly tested and updated to remain effective. Organizations should conduct periodic risk assessments, penetration testing, and security audits to identify new vulnerabilities and refine their risk management strategies. Security teams must stay informed about emerging threats, leveraging threat intelligence and real-time monitoring solutions to detect and respond to potential attacks proactively.

A strong cyber risk assessment methodology also requires collaboration between different departments within an organization. Risk assessments should not be confined to IT and security teams alone but should involve executive leadership, legal departments, compliance officers, and business units. Cyber risks impact various aspects of an organization, from financial stability to regulatory compliance, making it essential for all stakeholders to contribute to risk assessment efforts. Establishing clear communication channels and reporting mechanisms ensures that security risks are understood across the organization, enabling informed decision-making.

Cyber risk assessments must also account for third-party and supply chain risks. Organizations increasingly rely on third-party vendors, cloud service providers, and external partners, introducing additional security challenges. A comprehensive risk assessment should evaluate the security posture of external entities, requiring vendors to adhere to cybersecurity best practices and compliance standards. Organizations should establish vendor risk management programs that include contractual security requirements, regular security assessments, and continuous monitoring of third-party security controls.

As cyber threats continue to evolve, risk assessment methodologies must adapt to address emerging risks associated with artificial intelligence, the Internet of Things (IoT), and quantum computing. Organizations must integrate automation, machine learning, and advanced analytics into their risk assessment processes to enhance threat detection and response capabilities. Security frameworks must evolve to address new attack vectors, ensuring that organizations remain resilient against sophisticated cyber adversaries.

A well-executed cyber risk assessment methodology enables organizations to anticipate and mitigate cyber threats effectively. By implementing structured assessment frameworks, organizations can prioritize security investments, enhance regulatory compliance, and strengthen their overall security posture. Cyber risk assessments should be an ongoing effort, integrating real-time threat intelligence, continuous monitoring, and collaboration across all business functions. Organizations that proactively assess and manage cyber risks are better positioned to navigate the complexities of the modern threat landscape and maintain a secure and resilient digital environment.

Threat Modeling and Risk Prioritization

Threat modeling and risk prioritization are essential components of cybersecurity, enabling organizations to proactively identify, assess, and mitigate potential threats before they materialize into security incidents. In a constantly evolving digital landscape, organizations must adopt structured methodologies to evaluate the threats they face and allocate resources effectively to mitigate the most critical risks. Without a well-defined approach to threat modeling and risk prioritization, organizations may struggle to defend against cyberattacks, leading to financial losses, reputational damage, and operational disruptions.

Threat modeling is a systematic process used to identify and analyze potential threats to an organization's assets, applications, and systems. By understanding how attackers might exploit vulnerabilities, security teams can implement targeted defenses to reduce risk exposure. Threat modeling involves evaluating attack vectors, identifying security weaknesses, and assessing the potential impact of different threats. The goal is to anticipate how adversaries might compromise a system and take proactive measures to mitigate those risks before they can be exploited.

Several methodologies exist for performing threat modeling, each providing a structured framework for analyzing potential security threats. One widely used approach is the STRIDE model, developed by Microsoft, which categorizes threats into six types: Spoofing, Tampering, Repudiation, Information Disclosure, Denial of Service, and Elevation of Privilege. This model helps organizations systematically evaluate threats and determine how they might impact system security. Another common methodology is DREAD, which evaluates threats based on five factors: Damage potential, Reproducibility, Exploitability, Affected users, and Discoverability. This scoring system helps organizations prioritize threats based on their severity and likelihood of exploitation.

A more modern approach to threat modeling is the PASTA (Process for Attack Simulation and Threat Analysis) methodology, which integrates business impact analysis into the threat modeling process. Unlike traditional models that focus solely on technical vulnerabilities, PASTA aligns security threats with business objectives, helping organizations assess how cyber risks affect their overall operations. By combining threat intelligence, security analytics, and real-world attack scenarios, PASTA provides a dynamic and adaptive approach to threat modeling that evolves alongside emerging cyber threats.

Another essential methodology is the MITRE ATT&CK framework, which provides a comprehensive knowledge base of attacker tactics, techniques, and procedures (TTPs). By mapping potential attack scenarios against known adversary behaviors, organizations can develop more effective threat detection and response strategies. The MITRE ATT&CK framework is widely used by security operations centers (SOCs), red teams, and incident response teams to understand how attackers operate and enhance defensive measures accordingly.

Once threats are identified through threat modeling, the next critical step is risk prioritization. Organizations must assess which threats pose the greatest danger to their business and allocate security resources accordingly. Risk prioritization involves evaluating the likelihood and impact of each identified threat, ensuring that the most severe and probable risks receive immediate attention. Without proper risk prioritization, organizations may waste resources addressing low-risk threats while leaving critical vulnerabilities exposed.

Risk prioritization typically follows a structured approach, using risk assessment matrices and scoring systems to determine the severity of each threat. The risk matrix is a common tool that categorizes threats based on their likelihood (low, medium, high) and impact (minor, moderate, severe). Threats that fall into the high-likelihood and high-impact category require immediate mitigation, while lower-priority threats may be monitored or addressed through long-term security improvements. By using a risk matrix, organizations can visualize their risk landscape and make data-driven decisions about security investments.

Another effective approach to risk prioritization is quantitative risk assessment, which assigns numerical values to potential risks based on financial impact, system downtime, and data loss. The Factor Analysis of Information Risk (FAIR) model is one such framework that helps organizations quantify risk by evaluating variables such as threat event frequency, vulnerability probability, and loss magnitude. By translating cyber risks into financial terms, organizations can make more informed decisions about security budgets, insurance policies, and risk mitigation strategies.

Risk prioritization must also take into account the business context of each threat. Not all cyber risks have the same consequences for different organizations. For example, a data breach in a financial institution may have severe regulatory and reputational implications, whereas the same type of incident in a small startup might have a lower impact. Organizations must align risk prioritization with their specific industry, regulatory requirements, and business objectives. Executive leadership, legal teams, and compliance officers should be involved in risk prioritization discussions to ensure that cybersecurity initiatives align with overall corporate strategy.

Security automation and artificial intelligence (AI) have become valuable tools for enhancing threat modeling and risk prioritization. Modern security analytics platforms use AI-driven threat intelligence to detect emerging threats and predict attack patterns. By leveraging machine learning algorithms, organizations can automate risk scoring, identify anomalies, and prioritize threats in real time. Automated threat modeling tools can analyze security logs, network traffic, and endpoint behavior to provide continuous risk assessments without manual intervention. These technologies enable organizations to stay ahead of cyber threats by adapting their security posture based on evolving attack trends.

Collaboration between cybersecurity teams, developers, and business stakeholders is crucial for effective threat modeling and risk prioritization. Security teams must work closely with software developers to integrate security into the software development lifecycle (SDLC), ensuring that applications are designed with security in mind from the outset. DevSecOps practices encourage proactive threat modeling during the development process, reducing vulnerabilities before they reach production environments. Organizations that adopt a "shift-left" approach—incorporating security early in the development lifecycle—can significantly reduce security risks and lower the cost of remediation.

Regulatory and compliance requirements also play a role in risk prioritization. Organizations operating in highly regulated industries, such as healthcare, finance, and critical infrastructure, must prioritize threats that could lead to regulatory violations or legal consequences. Compliance frameworks such as GDPR, PCI DSS, HIPAA, and NIST provide guidelines for prioritizing security risks based on industry standards. By aligning risk prioritization with compliance requirements, organizations can avoid legal penalties and demonstrate due diligence in protecting sensitive data.

Threat modeling and risk prioritization must be ongoing processes that evolve with the changing cyber threat landscape. Cybercriminals continuously develop new attack techniques, making it essential for organizations to update their threat models and reassess risk priorities regularly. Security teams should conduct periodic red team exercises, penetration testing, and adversary simulations to validate the effectiveness of their risk prioritization strategies. Organizations that adopt a proactive and adaptive approach to threat modeling and risk prioritization can better protect their assets, reduce exposure to cyber threats, and strengthen their overall cybersecurity resilience.

Cybersecurity Policies and Procedures

Cybersecurity policies and procedures form the backbone of an organization's security framework, providing clear guidelines for protecting digital assets, managing risks, and responding to security incidents. These policies establish the rules and expectations for employees, contractors, and third-party vendors, ensuring that everyone adheres to security best practices. Without well-defined cybersecurity policies and procedures, organizations are vulnerable to data breaches, regulatory non-compliance, and operational disruptions. A strong cybersecurity policy framework enables organizations to maintain security consistency, minimize human error, and align security efforts with business objectives.

Cybersecurity policies serve as formal documents that outline an organization's security strategy, detailing the standards, controls, and practices necessary to safeguard sensitive data and IT infrastructure. These policies define the responsibilities of employees and IT teams, setting expectations for acceptable use, access management, incident response, and data protection. Policies must be tailored to the organization's industry, regulatory requirements, and risk tolerance. A well-structured cybersecurity policy framework ensures that security measures are applied uniformly across all departments and business units, reducing inconsistencies that attackers could exploit.

Procedures complement policies by providing step-by-step instructions for implementing security controls and responding to threats. While policies define the overarching security principles, procedures focus on the practical application of these principles. For example, an access control policy might state that employees must use strong authentication methods, while the corresponding procedure would outline the exact steps for setting up multi-factor authentication. Procedures ensure that security policies are actionable, enforceable, and integrated into daily business operations. Organizations must continuously review and update their procedures to keep pace with evolving threats and technological advancements.

One of the most critical cybersecurity policies is the acceptable use policy (AUP), which governs how employees, contractors, and third parties can use an organization's IT resources. The AUP defines the appropriate use of email, internet access, company devices, and software applications, prohibiting activities such as unauthorized data sharing, visiting malicious websites, or using unapproved software. This policy helps prevent security risks arising from careless or negligent behavior, ensuring that users follow cybersecurity best practices when interacting with corporate systems. AUP violations can lead to security breaches, making it essential for organizations to enforce compliance through monitoring and disciplinary actions.

Another essential cybersecurity policy is access control, which dictates how users authenticate and gain access to sensitive systems and data. Organizations must implement strict access control measures to prevent unauthorized access and limit exposure to cyber threats. The principle of least privilege (PoLP) is a core component of access control policies, ensuring that users only have access to the information necessary for their job functions. Role-based access control (RBAC) and mandatory access control (MAC) models help organizations enforce access restrictions based on user roles and security classifications. Multi-factor authentication (MFA) should be a mandatory requirement for accessing critical systems, reducing the risk of credential theft and unauthorized logins.

Data protection policies define how organizations handle sensitive information, including customer data, intellectual property, and financial records. These policies establish guidelines for data classification, encryption, and retention. Organizations must classify data based on sensitivity levels, such as public, internal, confidential, or highly restricted, ensuring that the appropriate security controls are applied. Encryption policies specify how data should be encrypted in transit and at rest, protecting it from unauthorized interception or theft. Data retention policies determine how long information should be stored and when it should be securely disposed of, reducing the risk of data exposure due to over-retention.

Incident response policies and procedures provide a structured approach to detecting, reporting, and mitigating security incidents. Organizations must have a clearly defined incident response plan (IRP) that outlines roles, escalation procedures, and communication protocols during a cyberattack. The IRP should include steps for containing threats, conducting forensic investigations, and restoring affected systems. Security teams must regularly conduct incident response drills and tabletop exercises to test the effectiveness of their procedures. Well-documented incident response procedures ensure that organizations can react quickly to cyber incidents, minimizing damage and maintaining business continuity.

Security awareness training policies mandate ongoing education for employees, helping them recognize cyber threats and follow security best practices. Human error is one of the leading causes of security breaches, making training a critical component of cybersecurity governance. Training policies should cover topics such as phishing awareness, password management, and secure data handling. Employees must learn how to identify social engineering tactics, avoid suspicious links, and report security incidents promptly. Organizations should conduct periodic training sessions and phishing simulations to reinforce security awareness across all levels of the organization.

Third-party risk management policies govern the security requirements for vendors, suppliers, and partners that have access to an organization's data or systems. Organizations increasingly rely on third-party service providers for cloud computing, software development, and IT outsourcing, introducing additional security risks. Third-party risk management policies must include vendor security assessments, contractual security requirements, and ongoing monitoring. Organizations should conduct due diligence before engaging with vendors, ensuring that they meet industry security standards and compliance requirements. Continuous monitoring of third-party security practices helps prevent supply chain attacks and data breaches originating from external partners.

Change management policies ensure that security is maintained when IT systems, applications, or infrastructure undergo modifications. Poorly managed changes can introduce vulnerabilities, misconfigurations, or system failures that attackers could exploit. Organizations must implement change control procedures that require security reviews, approvals, and testing before deploying changes to production environments. Change management policies should define processes for patch management, software updates, and system upgrades, ensuring that security risks are assessed before implementing changes. A well-structured change management framework minimizes the likelihood of security incidents caused by untested or unauthorized modifications.

Organizations must also establish compliance policies that align with regulatory requirements and industry standards. Compliance policies define how security controls are implemented to meet legal obligations, such as GDPR, HIPAA, PCI DSS, and NIST Cybersecurity Framework. These policies outline procedures for conducting security audits, maintaining documentation, and reporting compliance violations. Organizations must regularly review compliance policies to ensure alignment with evolving regulations and security best practices. Failure to adhere to compliance policies can result in legal penalties, financial fines, and reputational harm.

Cybersecurity policies and procedures must be continuously updated to address new threats, technologies, and regulatory changes. Organizations should conduct regular security policy reviews, risk assessments, and policy enforcement audits to identify gaps and improve security controls. Leadership teams must support cybersecurity initiatives by ensuring that policies are not just documents but actively enforced through security awareness programs, monitoring tools, and disciplinary actions. By developing and maintaining a strong cybersecurity policy framework, organizations can strengthen their security posture, protect sensitive information, and enhance overall cyber resilience in an increasingly complex threat landscape.

Regulatory Compliance in Cybersecurity

Regulatory compliance in cybersecurity is a critical component of an organization's risk management strategy, ensuring that businesses adhere to laws, standards, and best practices designed to protect sensitive data and digital infrastructure. As cyber threats continue to evolve, governments and regulatory bodies have introduced stringent cybersecurity laws to mitigate risks, prevent data breaches, and hold organizations accountable for protecting information assets. Failure to comply with regulatory requirements can result in severe financial penalties, legal consequences, and reputational damage, making compliance a fundamental aspect of cybersecurity governance.

The growing complexity of cybersecurity regulations is driven by the increasing frequency of cyberattacks and the need to protect personal, financial, and business data. Organizations operating in different industries and regions must comply with various legal frameworks that define how data should be collected, stored, processed, and transmitted. Compliance frameworks are designed to establish security baselines, ensuring that organizations implement appropriate security controls, conduct risk assessments, and maintain documentation for regulatory audits. The challenge for businesses is navigating the overlapping requirements of multiple regulations while maintaining an effective cybersecurity posture.

One of the most significant cybersecurity regulations is the General Data Protection Regulation (GDPR), which governs data privacy and protection in the European Union. GDPR imposes strict requirements on organizations that collect or process personal data of EU citizens, regardless of where the company is based. It mandates that businesses obtain explicit user consent for data processing, implement strong security measures to protect personal information, and report data breaches within 72 hours. Non-compliance with GDPR can result in fines of up to four percent of a company's global annual revenue, making it one of the most stringent data protection laws in the world.

The Health Insurance Portability and Accountability Act (HIPAA) in the United States is another crucial cybersecurity regulation, specifically targeting the healthcare industry. HIPAA requires healthcare providers, insurers, and business associates to implement security controls to protect electronic health records (EHRs) from unauthorized access and breaches. The law mandates encryption, access controls, audit logging, and employee training to ensure compliance. Organizations that fail to adhere to HIPAA regulations may face heavy fines and legal action, particularly if patient data is exposed due to negligence or cyberattacks.

For businesses handling payment card transactions, the Payment Card Industry Data Security Standard (PCI DSS) establishes security requirements to protect credit card information from fraud and theft. PCI DSS applies to merchants, payment processors, and financial institutions that store, process, or transmit payment card data. It requires organizations to implement strong encryption, secure authentication methods, and continuous monitoring of payment systems. Compliance with PCI DSS is crucial for preventing financial fraud, maintaining customer trust, and avoiding penalties from payment card brands such as Visa, Mastercard, and American Express.

The National Institute of Standards and Technology (NIST) Cybersecurity Framework provides a widely accepted set of guidelines for organizations to improve their cybersecurity resilience. While not legally mandated, many government agencies, defense contractors, and businesses use the NIST framework to establish risk-based security programs. The framework consists of five core functions: Identify, Protect, Detect, Respond, and Recover. These functions help organizations develop comprehensive security strategies that align with industry best practices and regulatory expectations. Many compliance programs integrate NIST recommendations as a benchmark for cybersecurity maturity assessments.

In the financial sector, the Sarbanes-Oxley Act (SOX) imposes cybersecurity and financial reporting requirements to ensure the integrity of corporate financial statements. SOX compliance mandates that publicly traded companies implement internal controls to safeguard financial data against cyber threats. Companies must conduct security audits, maintain secure access controls, and document risk management processes. Non-compliance with SOX can lead to criminal penalties for executives and financial losses due to regulatory fines and investor lawsuits.

Cloud computing has introduced additional compliance challenges, as organizations increasingly rely on third-party cloud service providers to store and process sensitive data. Regulations such as SOC 2 (Service Organization Control 2) establish security and privacy criteria for cloud providers, requiring them to implement security controls related to confidentiality, availability, and data integrity. Businesses that use cloud services must ensure that their providers adhere to compliance standards, conducting regular security assessments and contractual reviews to mitigate third-party risks.

Many governments have introduced national cybersecurity laws to address growing concerns over cyber espionage, critical infrastructure security, and digital privacy. The Cybersecurity Maturity Model Certification (CMMC), developed by the U.S. Department of Defense, sets cybersecurity requirements for defense contractors to protect classified and sensitive government data. Similarly, China's Cybersecurity Law (CSL) imposes strict data localization and security measures for businesses operating within its jurisdiction. The evolving regulatory landscape requires organizations to stay informed about international cybersecurity laws that may impact their operations and supply chain security.

Compliance with cybersecurity regulations requires organizations to implement a structured approach that includes risk assessments, policy enforcement, employee training, and continuous monitoring. A robust compliance strategy begins with identifying applicable regulations based on industry, geography, and business operations.

Organizations must conduct compliance gap assessments to evaluate their current security posture and identify areas that require improvement. Security policies should be developed to align with regulatory requirements, ensuring that data protection measures, incident response plans, and access controls meet compliance obligations.

Regulatory audits play a key role in verifying cybersecurity compliance. Organizations must maintain detailed documentation of their security policies, risk management processes, and incident response procedures to demonstrate compliance during audits. Internal and external audits help identify weaknesses, assess compliance levels, and ensure that security controls are effectively implemented. Many regulatory bodies require organizations to undergo third-party security assessments to validate compliance, reinforcing the importance of maintaining up-to-date security documentation.

Security awareness training is a crucial element of regulatory compliance, as human error remains one of the leading causes of data breaches. Compliance programs should include mandatory cybersecurity training for employees, educating them on data protection requirements, phishing prevention, and secure handling of sensitive information. Organizations must also establish incident reporting procedures, ensuring that security incidents are promptly identified, escalated, and mitigated in accordance with regulatory guidelines.

The future of regulatory compliance in cybersecurity will continue to evolve as governments introduce new laws to address emerging threats such as ransomware, supply chain attacks, and artificial intelligence-driven cybercrime. Organizations must adopt a proactive approach to compliance, staying informed about legislative changes and integrating security best practices into their operations. Compliance should not be viewed as a one-time effort but as a continuous process that enhances overall cybersecurity resilience. By embedding compliance into their security strategies, organizations can protect sensitive data, reduce legal risks, and build trust with customers and stakeholders in an increasingly digital world.

Industry-Specific Compliance Requirements

Industry-specific compliance requirements play a crucial role in cybersecurity by ensuring that organizations adhere to security standards and regulations tailored to their sector. Different industries have unique cybersecurity challenges based on the types of data they handle, the threats they face, and the regulatory bodies overseeing them. Compliance frameworks establish guidelines for protecting sensitive information, preventing cyber threats, and maintaining the integrity of digital systems. Businesses that fail to meet these compliance requirements risk financial penalties, reputational damage, and legal consequences. Adhering to industry-specific regulations helps organizations build trust with customers, partners, and stakeholders by demonstrating a commitment to cybersecurity best practices.

The healthcare industry is one of the most highly regulated sectors when it comes to cybersecurity compliance. The Health Insurance Portability and Accountability Act (HIPAA) in the United States establishes strict security and privacy requirements for healthcare providers, insurers, and business associates that handle electronic protected health information (ePHI). HIPAA mandates that organizations implement administrative, technical, and physical safeguards to protect patient data from unauthorized access, breaches, and cyberattacks. Compliance with HIPAA requires encryption of sensitive information, secure access controls, and regular risk assessments to identify vulnerabilities. Organizations that fail to meet HIPAA standards face substantial fines and legal penalties, particularly if a data breach results in the exposure of patient records. Similar regulations exist in other regions, such as the General Data Protection Regulation (GDPR) in the European Union, which includes specific provisions for protecting health-related data.

The financial sector also operates under stringent cybersecurity compliance requirements due to the high value of financial data and the risk of fraud. Regulations such as the Payment Card Industry Data Security Standard (PCI DSS) set strict security guidelines for organizations that handle credit card transactions. PCI DSS requires businesses to implement encryption, network segmentation, access controls, and continuous monitoring to prevent payment card fraud. Financial institutions must also comply with the Sarbanes-Oxley Act (SOX), which mandates internal controls and security measures to ensure the integrity of financial reporting. Additionally, the Gramm-Leach-Bliley Act (GLBA) requires financial institutions to implement safeguards for protecting customer financial information. Regulatory bodies such as the U.S. Office of the Comptroller of the Currency (OCC) and the Financial Industry Regulatory Authority (FINRA) enforce compliance within the financial sector, ensuring that organizations adopt robust cybersecurity controls to prevent fraud, insider threats, and cyberattacks.

The energy and utilities sector is considered critical infrastructure and is subject to specific cybersecurity compliance regulations to ensure operational security and resilience. In the United States, the North American Electric Reliability Corporation Critical Infrastructure Protection (NERC CIP) standards outline security requirements for protecting bulk electric system assets from cyber threats. NERC CIP mandates security controls for access management, incident response, system monitoring, and risk assessments. The goal is to prevent cyberattacks that could disrupt power grids, water treatment facilities, and other essential services. In Europe, the Network and Information Security (NIS) Directive sets cybersecurity requirements for critical infrastructure providers, ensuring that energy, transport, and healthcare sectors maintain strong security postures. Organizations in the energy sector must also comply with industrial cybersecurity standards such as ISO/IEC 27019, which provides guidelines for securing energy control systems.

The defense and government sectors have some of the most rigorous cybersecurity compliance requirements due to national security concerns. Contractors working with the U.S. Department of Defense (DoD) must comply with the Cybersecurity Maturity Model Certification (CMMC) framework, which establishes security requirements based on the sensitivity of government contracts. CMMC requires defense contractors to implement access controls, endpoint security, encryption, and continuous monitoring to protect classified and unclassified government data. In addition to CMMC, organizations handling government data must comply with the Federal

Information Security Modernization Act (FISMA), which outlines security standards for federal agencies and their contractors. Similar regulations exist in other countries, such as the UK Cyber Essentials Scheme and Australia's Information Security Manual (ISM), ensuring that government-related data remains protected from cyber threats.

Retail and e-commerce businesses face cybersecurity compliance requirements to protect consumer data and prevent online fraud. The PCI DSS framework applies to retailers that process credit card payments, requiring them to implement secure authentication, firewalls, and monitoring tools to prevent payment data breaches. The California Consumer Privacy Act (CCPA) and GDPR impose strict data privacy requirements on e-commerce businesses, mandating that companies inform customers about data collection practices and provide them with options to control their personal information. Failure to comply with these regulations can result in lawsuits, financial penalties, and damage to brand reputation. Retailers must also implement strong fraud detection measures, secure web applications, and anti-malware protections to safeguard online transactions and customer data.

The telecommunications sector is responsible for securing vast amounts of customer data and critical communication networks. Telecommunications companies must comply with regulations such as the Telecommunications Act, which mandates data protection measures and consumer privacy safeguards. In Europe, the Electronic Communications Code (ECC) requires telecom providers to implement cybersecurity measures to protect user communications from cyber threats. The Federal Communications Commission (FCC) in the United States enforces compliance with data protection laws for telecom providers, ensuring that sensitive customer information remains secure. Telecom companies must also implement security measures to prevent Distributed Denial of Service (DDoS) attacks, insider threats, and supply chain vulnerabilities that could compromise network integrity.

Manufacturing and industrial sectors have specific cybersecurity compliance requirements due to the rise of Industrial Control Systems (ICS) and Operational Technology (OT) networks. The International Society of Automation (ISA)/International Electrotechnical

Commission (IEC) 62443 standard provides cybersecurity guidelines for securing ICS environments, ensuring that manufacturing systems are protected from cyberattacks that could disrupt production lines and supply chains. Organizations in this sector must also comply with NIST standards and industry-specific guidelines that mandate security controls for protecting industrial networks and automation systems. As cyber threats targeting industrial infrastructure increase, compliance with ICS security standards has become essential for maintaining operational continuity and preventing cyber-physical attacks.

The education sector also faces cybersecurity compliance requirements, particularly when handling student and research data. In the United States, the Family Educational Rights and Privacy Act (FERPA) establishes privacy protections for student records, requiring educational institutions to implement security controls that prevent unauthorized access. The Children's Online Privacy Protection Act (COPPA) mandates that organizations collecting personal information from children under 13 comply with strict data privacy guidelines. Universities and research institutions must also protect intellectual property and research data from cyber espionage, requiring strong access controls, data encryption, and cybersecurity training programs for faculty and students.

Each industry has its own cybersecurity compliance requirements tailored to its risks, operational needs, and regulatory landscape. Organizations must continuously monitor regulatory updates, conduct compliance audits, and implement security best practices to meet industry-specific security obligations. Regulatory compliance not only helps organizations avoid legal penalties but also strengthens cybersecurity resilience, ensuring that sensitive data and critical infrastructure remain protected from cyber threats. As cyber risks continue to evolve, industries must adapt their compliance strategies to address new security challenges and regulatory developments.

Third-Party Risk Management

Third-party risk management (TPRM) is a critical aspect of cybersecurity, as organizations increasingly rely on external vendors, suppliers, contractors, and service providers to support business operations. While third parties offer essential services and technological advancements, they also introduce significant security risks, as they often have access to sensitive data, internal systems, and infrastructure. A weak security posture from a third-party partner can become an entry point for cyber attackers, leading to data breaches, regulatory violations, and operational disruptions. Organizations must establish comprehensive third-party risk management programs to identify, assess, and mitigate these risks effectively.

As businesses expand their digital ecosystems, third-party relationships have become more complex, involving cloud service providers, software vendors, outsourced IT teams, and business process outsourcing (BPO) companies. These external entities may handle customer data, financial transactions, intellectual property, or critical infrastructure, making them attractive targets for cybercriminals. Attackers often exploit weak security controls within third-party networks to gain unauthorized access to a company's systems. A well-known example is the 2013 Target data breach, where attackers compromised a third-party HVAC vendor to gain access to the retailer's network, leading to the exposure of millions of customer records. Such incidents highlight the need for organizations to implement rigorous security assessments and monitoring mechanisms for their third-party relationships.

A robust third-party risk management framework begins with vendor risk assessments, where organizations evaluate the security posture of potential third-party partners before entering into a business relationship. This assessment should include a review of the vendor's security policies, data protection practices, compliance certifications, and past security incidents. Organizations should require vendors to complete security questionnaires, provide evidence of cybersecurity controls, and conduct vulnerability assessments to ensure they meet industry security standards. Risk assessments should also consider the level of access granted to third parties, ensuring that vendors have only the minimum necessary access to perform their functions, following the principle of least privilege.

Once a vendor is onboarded, organizations must establish contractual security requirements to enforce compliance with cybersecurity policies and regulatory obligations. Vendor contracts should include clauses that outline data protection responsibilities, security controls, breach notification requirements, and compliance obligations. Organizations should also include provisions for conducting security audits, requiring third parties to undergo periodic assessments to verify their adherence to security best practices. In industries with strict regulatory requirements, such as healthcare, finance, and government contracting, vendors must demonstrate compliance with frameworks like GDPR, HIPAA, PCI DSS, SOC 2, and NIST 800-171.

Continuous monitoring is a key component of third-party risk management, as security risks evolve over time. Organizations cannot rely solely on pre-engagement assessments but must implement ongoing vendor security monitoring to detect emerging threats. Automated security tools, such as Security Information and Event Management (SIEM) systems, threat intelligence platforms, and risk-scoring solutions, provide real-time insights into third-party security risks. Organizations should monitor vendor access logs, detect anomalous activity, and review security performance metrics to identify potential vulnerabilities. Regular penetration testing and vulnerability scans of vendor systems help ensure that security controls remain effective throughout the partnership.

Incident response planning must also extend to third-party relationships. Organizations should require vendors to have incident response plans (IRPs) in place and establish clear protocols for handling security incidents that impact shared systems or data. Third parties should be required to notify organizations immediately in the event of a data breach, unauthorized access, or security misconfiguration. Collaborative incident response drills and tabletop exercises can help organizations and their vendors coordinate actions during a cybersecurity event, ensuring that response efforts are swift and effective. Organizations should also define remediation requirements in their contracts, ensuring that vendors take corrective actions promptly in case of security failures.

Data security and privacy protection are particularly important when third parties handle sensitive information. Organizations should enforce data encryption policies, secure data transmission protocols, and access controls to prevent unauthorized access or data leaks. Zero-trust security models can enhance third-party risk management by requiring continuous authentication and verification for all external users and systems. Organizations should also establish data loss prevention (DLP) solutions to monitor and control how third-party vendors interact with sensitive information.

Cloud service providers present unique challenges in third-party risk management, as they store and process vast amounts of corporate and customer data. Organizations must assess cloud security controls, shared responsibility models, and compliance certifications before engaging with cloud vendors. Multi-cloud security strategies, identity and access management (IAM) solutions, and encryption protocols should be implemented to protect cloud-based data. Organizations should also ensure that cloud vendors comply with regulatory frameworks such as ISO 27001, SOC 2, FedRAMP, and CSA STAR, which provide standardized security controls for cloud environments.

Fourth-party risk management is an emerging area of concern, as third-party vendors often subcontract services to additional external entities. Organizations must extend security assessments beyond direct vendors to include their subcontractors and supply chain partners. Supply chain attacks, such as the SolarWinds breach, demonstrate how attackers can compromise a vendor's software updates to infiltrate multiple organizations. Organizations should require vendors to disclose their subcontracting relationships and enforce security standards across the extended supply chain to minimize risks.

Employee awareness and training are also essential for effective third-party risk management. Organizations should educate employees on the security risks associated with third-party access, phishing threats, and supply chain vulnerabilities. Security teams must conduct regular audits and review vendor access permissions to ensure that external entities do not retain unnecessary access to systems after contract termination. Organizations should establish clear offboarding procedures to revoke vendor credentials, disable shared accounts, and retrieve company-owned devices or data when a third-party relationship ends.

Regulatory compliance plays a significant role in third-party risk management, as organizations are legally responsible for ensuring that their vendors comply with cybersecurity laws and industry standards. Regulators increasingly hold companies accountable for third-party security failures, making it essential for businesses to document risk assessments, security audits, and compliance reports. Due diligence and contractual security measures help organizations demonstrate regulatory compliance and reduce legal liabilities related to third-party cybersecurity incidents.

Third-party risk management requires a proactive and structured approach to assess, monitor, and mitigate security risks associated with external vendors. Organizations must implement vendor risk assessments, contractual security controls, continuous monitoring, and incident response planning to protect their data and systems. By enforcing security best practices, regulatory compliance, and zero-trust security models, businesses can minimize the risks posed by third-party relationships and strengthen their overall cybersecurity posture. Effective third-party risk management not only reduces vulnerabilities but also enhances trust and security across the entire digital supply chain.

Cybersecurity Frameworks: NIST, ISO, CIS

Cybersecurity frameworks provide structured guidelines for organizations to manage security risks, implement effective controls, and ensure compliance with industry standards. Among the most widely recognized frameworks are the National Institute of Standards and Technology (NIST) Cybersecurity Framework (CSF), the International Organization for Standardization (ISO) 27001, and the Center for Internet Security (CIS) Controls. These frameworks help organizations of all sizes build robust security postures by defining best practices, establishing risk management processes, and aligning security efforts with business objectives. While each framework has its unique approach, they all serve a common goal: improving cybersecurity resilience against evolving threats.

The NIST Cybersecurity Framework (CSF) was developed by the U.S. National Institute of Standards and Technology to provide organizations with a flexible, risk-based approach to managing cybersecurity. Originally designed for critical infrastructure sectors, NIST CSF has gained widespread adoption across industries due to its adaptability and structured methodology. The framework consists of five core functions: Identify, Protect, Detect, Respond, and Recover. These functions provide a structured approach for organizations to assess their security posture, implement protective measures, monitor for threats, respond to incidents, and ensure business continuity.

The Identify function focuses on understanding cybersecurity risks, including asset management, business environment analysis, governance, and risk assessments. Organizations must establish visibility into their IT infrastructure, data flows, and security dependencies to effectively manage cyber risks. The Protect function involves implementing security controls such as access management, data protection, and security awareness training to reduce the likelihood of a breach. The Detect function emphasizes continuous monitoring, intrusion detection, and security analytics to identify potential threats in real time. The Respond function ensures that organizations have well-defined incident response plans, communication strategies, and mitigation procedures in place. The Recover function focuses on business continuity planning and disaster recovery to restore operations after a security incident.

One of the key advantages of NIST CSF is its flexibility. Unlike prescriptive standards, the framework allows organizations to customize security controls based on their unique risk profiles and business priorities. NIST CSF also aligns with other cybersecurity regulations and frameworks, including ISO 27001, CIS Controls, HIPAA, and PCI DSS, making it a valuable tool for regulatory compliance. Organizations use NIST CSF as a baseline for security assessments, risk management, and continuous improvement initiatives.

The ISO/IEC 27001 standard is a globally recognized framework for information security management systems (ISMS). Developed by the International Organization for Standardization (ISO) and the International Electrotechnical Commission (IEC), ISO 27001 provides a comprehensive set of security controls and risk management principles that organizations can implement to protect sensitive data. The standard follows a risk-based approach, requiring organizations to assess security threats, implement mitigation measures, and continuously improve security processes.

ISO 27001 is structured around the Plan-Do-Check-Act (PDCA) model, which ensures a systematic approach to information security management. The Plan phase involves risk assessments, defining security policies, and establishing governance structures. The Do phase includes implementing security controls, training employees, and deploying cybersecurity technologies. The Check phase focuses on monitoring security performance, conducting audits, and assessing the effectiveness of security controls. The Act phase ensures that organizations continuously improve their security posture by addressing vulnerabilities, updating policies, and responding to new threats.

ISO 27001 is widely used in industries that handle sensitive customer data, intellectual property, and financial transactions. Organizations that achieve ISO 27001 certification demonstrate their commitment to security best practices and regulatory compliance. The certification process involves an independent audit, where accredited assessors evaluate an organization's security policies, risk management framework, and control implementations. ISO 27001 certification is often required by business partners, regulators, and customers as proof of strong cybersecurity measures.

The Center for Internet Security (CIS) Controls is another widely adopted cybersecurity framework that provides a set of prioritized security measures to defend against cyber threats. CIS Controls are designed to help organizations mitigate the most common attack vectors by implementing practical and cost-effective security measures. The CIS framework consists of 18 security controls, categorized into three implementation groups based on an organization's size, risk profile, and security maturity.

CIS Controls are structured in a prioritized manner, meaning that organizations should implement foundational controls first before advancing to more complex security measures. The first six controls, known as the Basic Controls, include inventory and control of assets, secure configuration management, vulnerability management, controlled use of administrative privileges, and monitoring of security logs. These controls provide a strong foundation for preventing common security incidents such as unauthorized access, malware infections, and misconfigurations.

The Foundational Controls address network security, email protection, data recovery, and endpoint security. These measures ensure that organizations deploy secure system configurations, protect communication channels, and implement secure backup solutions. The Organizational Controls focus on security awareness training, incident response planning, penetration testing, and security governance. These controls help organizations build a security culture, prepare for cyber incidents, and continuously assess their security defenses.

One of the key benefits of CIS Controls is their practicality and alignment with real-world cyber threats. Unlike more general frameworks, CIS Controls are based on empirical threat data and cybersecurity incidents, ensuring that organizations address the most pressing security risks. The framework also integrates with NIST, ISO 27001, and regulatory compliance requirements, making it a valuable tool for organizations seeking a structured approach to security improvement.

Each of these cybersecurity frameworks offers unique advantages, and organizations often combine elements from multiple frameworks to create a customized security strategy. For example, a financial institution may use NIST CSF to assess its overall cybersecurity maturity, adopt ISO 27001 for managing security policies and governance, and implement CIS Controls to address specific attack vectors. The ability to integrate multiple frameworks allows organizations to build a resilient cybersecurity program tailored to their risk landscape and regulatory requirements.

Cybersecurity frameworks such as NIST CSF, ISO 27001, and CIS Controls provide organizations with structured methodologies for managing security risks, improving threat detection, and ensuring compliance with industry best practices. Each framework offers a unique perspective on cybersecurity governance, risk management, and security controls, helping organizations strengthen their defense against cyber threats. By implementing and adapting these frameworks, businesses can create a robust cybersecurity foundation that evolves alongside emerging threats and technological advancements.

GDPR and Data Privacy Regulations

The General Data Protection Regulation (GDPR) is one of the most comprehensive and influential data privacy laws in the world. Enforced by the European Union (EU) since May 25, 2018, GDPR establishes strict guidelines for the collection, processing, storage, and transfer of personal data. Its primary goal is to protect the privacy rights of EU citizens and residents by giving them greater control over their personal information. GDPR applies to any organization that processes the personal data of individuals in the EU, regardless of whether the organization is based within the EU. This extraterritorial scope makes GDPR a global standard for data privacy and has influenced privacy laws in other regions.

One of the core principles of GDPR is lawfulness, fairness, and transparency, which requires organizations to process personal data in a legal, ethical, and open manner. Businesses must ensure that data collection and processing activities have a legitimate basis, such as user consent, contractual necessity, legal obligation, protection of vital interests, public task, or legitimate interest. Organizations must inform individuals about how their data is being used, who has access to it, and how long it will be retained. GDPR mandates that privacy policies and terms of service be written in clear and simple language to enhance transparency.

The principle of data minimization ensures that organizations collect only the data necessary for a specific purpose. Under GDPR, businesses cannot gather excessive personal information beyond what is required for their stated purpose. Similarly, the storage limitation principle dictates that personal data should not be retained for longer than necessary. Organizations must define data retention policies and implement secure deletion methods to dispose of outdated or unnecessary personal information.

A fundamental right granted by GDPR is the right to access and portability, which allows individuals to request a copy of their personal data held by an organization. Businesses must provide this information in a structured, commonly used, and machine-readable format to enable data portability. The right to rectification allows individuals to correct inaccurate or incomplete data, while the right to erasure, also known as the "right to be forgotten," permits individuals to request the deletion of their data under certain circumstances. These rights empower users to maintain control over their digital footprint and request changes to their personal information.

GDPR also introduces strict rules for data processing by third parties and international data transfers. Organizations must ensure that any third-party processors handling personal data comply with GDPR's security and privacy standards. This is particularly important for cloud service providers, marketing agencies, and outsourced IT teams that process customer data on behalf of businesses. International data transfers outside the EU are only allowed if the receiving country has adequate data protection laws or if the organization uses Standard Contractual Clauses (SCCs), Binding Corporate Rules (BCRs), or other legal mechanisms approved by the EU. The invalidation of the Privacy Shield framework in 2020 forced many companies to reassess their data transfer mechanisms, increasing the complexity of global data compliance.

Another critical aspect of GDPR is its security and breach notification requirements. Organizations must implement technical and organizational measures to protect personal data from unauthorized access, loss, or theft. Security measures include encryption, pseudonymization, multi-factor authentication, and access controls. GDPR mandates that organizations report data breaches to supervisory authorities within 72 hours of becoming aware of an incident. If a breach poses a significant risk to individuals' rights, affected individuals must also be informed promptly. Failure to report a breach within the required timeframe can result in significant penalties.

One of the most well-known aspects of GDPR is its strict enforcement and severe penalties. Organizations found in violation of GDPR face fines of up to €20 million or 4% of their global annual revenue, whichever is higher. These fines are applied based on the severity of the violation, the level of negligence, the impact on affected individuals, and whether corrective actions were taken. High-profile cases, such as fines against Google, Facebook, and Amazon, demonstrate that regulators actively enforce GDPR to ensure compliance. The financial and reputational risks associated with GDPR violations have prompted businesses worldwide to strengthen their data protection practices.

GDPR has influenced other privacy regulations across the globe. Countries such as Brazil, Canada, India, Japan, and South Korea have introduced or updated their data protection laws to align with GDPR principles. In the United States, states like California, Virginia, and Colorado have implemented comprehensive privacy laws that grant individuals greater control over their data. The California Consumer Privacy Act (CCPA) and its successor, the California Privacy Rights Act (CPRA), introduce GDPR-like rights for consumers, such as the ability to opt out of data sales and request access to personal data. These laws signal a broader shift toward stricter data privacy regulations worldwide.

Compliance with GDPR requires organizations to take a proactive approach to data governance. Businesses must conduct Data Protection Impact Assessments (DPIAs) to evaluate the risks associated with data processing activities. They must also appoint a Data Protection Officer (DPO) if they process large volumes of sensitive data or monitor individuals on a large scale. The DPO serves as an internal expert on GDPR compliance, ensuring that the organization adheres to data protection laws and best practices.

Employee training and awareness programs are essential for maintaining GDPR compliance. Organizations must educate employees on data handling procedures, privacy policies, security best practices, and breach response protocols. Many data breaches occur due to human error, such as misconfigured databases, accidental disclosures, or weak password management. Regular training sessions help mitigate these risks by ensuring that employees understand their responsibilities under GDPR.

The rise of emerging technologies, such as artificial intelligence (AI), machine learning, and biometric authentication, presents new challenges for GDPR compliance. AI-driven decision-making systems that process personal data must adhere to GDPR's transparency and accountability requirements. Organizations using AI must ensure that individuals can understand and challenge automated decisions that affect them. Similarly, biometric data, such as fingerprints and facial recognition, is classified as special category data under GDPR and requires additional safeguards.

GDPR and data privacy regulations continue to evolve as digital transformation accelerates and new cyber threats emerge. Regulatory bodies frequently update their guidance and enforcement priorities, requiring organizations to stay informed and adapt their data protection strategies. Businesses that embed privacy by design and by default into their operations will not only achieve compliance but also gain a competitive advantage by building trust with customers and stakeholders. Strong data privacy practices enhance brand reputation, reduce legal risks, and improve overall cybersecurity resilience in an increasingly data-driven world.

PCI DSS Compliance for Financial Security

The Payment Card Industry Data Security Standard (PCI DSS) is a globally recognized security framework designed to protect payment card data and reduce the risk of fraud and cyberattacks. It was established by the Payment Card Industry Security Standards Council (PCI SSC), which includes major credit card brands such as Visa, Mastercard, American Express, Discover, and JCB. PCI DSS compliance is required for any organization that processes, stores, or transmits cardholder data, including merchants, financial institutions, and payment service providers. The standard outlines a comprehensive set of security controls to ensure the confidentiality, integrity, and security of payment card transactions.

PCI DSS consists of 12 core security requirements, which are organized into six categories. These requirements address key areas of financial security, including network protection, data encryption, access control, and vulnerability management. The first category focuses on building and maintaining a secure network, requiring organizations to configure firewalls, avoid using vendor-supplied default passwords, and implement strong authentication mechanisms. Firewalls serve as a critical barrier between external threats and internal payment systems, preventing unauthorized access. Changing default passwords and security settings is essential, as attackers frequently exploit weak or unchanged credentials to gain entry into systems.

Another critical aspect of PCI DSS is the protection of cardholder data, which includes both primary account numbers (PANs) and sensitive authentication data such as card verification codes (CVV) and expiration dates. Organizations must use encryption and tokenization to protect cardholder data at rest and in transit. Encryption ensures that payment data remains unreadable to unauthorized parties, while tokenization replaces sensitive card details with randomly generated tokens that have no exploitable value. These techniques help mitigate the risk of data breaches and unauthorized access to payment information.

To maintain financial security, PCI DSS requires organizations to implement strong access control measures. Only authorized personnel should have access to payment data, and organizations must follow the principle of least privilege (PoLP) to minimize exposure. Multi-factor authentication (MFA) is a key security measure that enhances access control by requiring users to verify their identity using multiple authentication factors, such as passwords, biometrics, or one-time codes. Organizations must also maintain unique user IDs and detailed access logs to track and monitor system activity, ensuring that only authorized individuals access payment data.

Vulnerability management is another fundamental component of PCI DSS compliance. Organizations must implement regular security updates, patch management, and vulnerability scans to identify and remediate weaknesses in their payment systems. Cybercriminals often exploit outdated software and unpatched vulnerabilities to gain unauthorized access to sensitive data. PCI DSS mandates that organizations conduct quarterly vulnerability scans and annual penetration testing to assess their security posture and detect potential attack vectors. These proactive security measures help organizations stay ahead of emerging threats and reinforce their financial security infrastructure.

PCI DSS also emphasizes the importance of monitoring and testing security systems to detect anomalies and prevent fraud. Organizations must deploy intrusion detection and prevention systems (IDS/IPS) to identify malicious activity and respond to security incidents in real time. Security event logging and centralized log management are required to track system activity and detect unauthorized access attempts. Organizations must review security logs regularly and implement automated threat detection tools to analyze patterns and detect suspicious behavior. Real-time monitoring allows security teams to respond swiftly to potential breaches and mitigate risks before they escalate.

Maintaining a comprehensive information security policy is a key requirement of PCI DSS compliance. Organizations must establish security policies that define roles, responsibilities, and procedures for protecting payment card data. Employee security awareness training is also essential, as human error is a common factor in security breaches. Regular training sessions should educate employees on phishing threats, social engineering tactics, and best practices for handling payment card data. Ensuring that staff members understand PCI DSS requirements helps organizations strengthen their overall security posture and prevent accidental data exposures.

Compliance with PCI DSS is not a one-time effort but an ongoing process that requires continuous evaluation and improvement. Organizations must conduct regular compliance assessments and audits to verify adherence to PCI DSS requirements. The level of assessment required depends on the organization's size, transaction volume, and risk profile. Large organizations and financial institutions may be required to undergo an annual PCI DSS assessment by a Qualified Security Assessor (QSA), while smaller businesses may complete a Self-Assessment Questionnaire (SAQ) to validate their compliance.

Failure to comply with PCI DSS can result in severe financial and reputational consequences. Organizations that experience a data breach due to non-compliance may face hefty fines from payment card brands, legal liabilities, and potential lawsuits. Non-compliant businesses may also lose the ability to process credit card transactions, damaging their ability to operate effectively. Beyond regulatory penalties, data breaches can erode customer trust and lead to long-term reputational damage. Organizations that invest in PCI DSS compliance demonstrate a commitment to protecting customer payment data and reducing the risk of fraud.

The growing adoption of contactless payments, e-commerce transactions, and mobile payment applications presents new challenges for PCI DSS compliance. Cybercriminals frequently target digital payment systems, making it essential for organizations to implement secure application development practices, endpoint protection, and fraud prevention measures. Organizations must ensure that mobile and online payment platforms adhere to PCI DSS security controls, including secure coding practices, encryption, and vulnerability testing. As financial technology evolves, PCI DSS requirements continue to adapt to address emerging threats and new payment processing technologies.

Cloud computing and third-party payment processors introduce additional considerations for PCI DSS compliance. Organizations that outsource payment processing to third-party vendors must ensure that their providers are PCI DSS certified and adhere to security best practices. Businesses should conduct due diligence, security assessments, and contractual agreements to verify that third-party vendors maintain robust security controls. The shared responsibility model in cloud environments requires organizations to define clear security responsibilities between cloud providers and customers, ensuring that PCI DSS requirements are met at every level.

PCI DSS compliance is a fundamental requirement for financial security, protecting payment card data from cyber threats and fraud. By implementing strong encryption, access controls, vulnerability management, and security monitoring, organizations can reduce the risk of data breaches and maintain the integrity of their payment systems. Continuous compliance efforts, regular security assessments, employee training, and third-party risk management are essential to sustaining a secure payment environment. As cyber threats continue to evolve, organizations must remain vigilant and proactive in their approach to PCI DSS compliance, ensuring that they safeguard financial transactions and maintain customer trust.

SOC 2 and Cloud Security Compliance

SOC 2 compliance plays a crucial role in cloud security, ensuring that cloud service providers and organizations handling sensitive data adhere to strict security, privacy, and operational controls. Developed by the American Institute of Certified Public Accountants (AICPA), SOC 2 (Service Organization Control 2) is a widely recognized framework that evaluates how service providers manage customer data based on five trust service criteria: security, availability, processing integrity, confidentiality, and privacy. As cloud computing adoption continues to rise, organizations must ensure that their cloud service providers comply with SOC 2 to protect sensitive data, maintain regulatory compliance, and mitigate cybersecurity risks.

SOC 2 compliance is particularly relevant for Software as a Service (SaaS) providers, cloud storage providers, financial institutions, healthcare organizations, and managed service providers that handle customer information. Unlike prescriptive compliance frameworks that define specific security controls, SOC 2 allows organizations to implement their own security practices, provided they meet the overarching trust service criteria. This flexibility enables companies to align SOC 2 compliance with their unique security requirements while demonstrating adherence to industry best practices.

The security criterion is the foundation of SOC 2 compliance, ensuring that an organization implements strong security controls to protect data from unauthorized access, breaches, and cyber threats. Security controls include firewalls, intrusion detection systems, encryption, multi-factor authentication (MFA), and access control mechanisms. Organizations must demonstrate that they have effective security monitoring and incident response capabilities to detect and mitigate threats in real time. The use of security information and event management (SIEM) tools, endpoint detection and response (EDR) solutions, and threat intelligence feeds helps organizations enhance their security posture and comply with SOC 2 security requirements.

The availability criterion focuses on ensuring that systems and services remain operational and accessible to customers. Organizations must implement business continuity and disaster recovery (BC/DR) plans, redundancy measures, and uptime monitoring to prevent service disruptions. Cloud service providers must demonstrate their ability to maintain high availability, scalability, and resilience while minimizing downtime. Service level agreements (SLAs) often include SOC 2 availability commitments, ensuring that customers receive reliable and uninterrupted services. Regular stress testing, failover testing, and infrastructure monitoring help organizations maintain compliance with SOC 2 availability requirements.

The processing integrity criterion ensures that data is processed accurately, completely, and in a timely manner. Organizations must implement quality control measures, error detection systems, and transaction monitoring to prevent unauthorized modifications or corruption of data. Cloud providers handling financial transactions, healthcare records, or legal documents must establish data validation, logging, and audit mechanisms to verify that information is processed correctly. Processing integrity compliance requires automated testing, workflow monitoring, and system validations to maintain the integrity of digital transactions.

The confidentiality criterion focuses on protecting sensitive data from unauthorized access and disclosure. Organizations must enforce data classification policies, role-based access control (RBAC), and secure data transmission protocols to prevent data leaks. Cloud providers handling intellectual property, proprietary business information, and financial records must implement encryption at rest and in transit, data loss prevention (DLP) solutions, and restricted access policies. SOC 2 audits assess whether organizations have strong access management, logging, and encryption policies to protect confidential data.

The privacy criterion ensures that organizations collect, store, and process personal data in compliance with data protection regulations such as GDPR, CCPA, and HIPAA. SOC 2 privacy compliance requires organizations to define data retention policies, consent management mechanisms, and data subject rights procedures. Organizations must demonstrate secure data handling, anonymization, and privacy impact assessments (PIAs) to comply with SOC 2 privacy requirements. Businesses that handle customer data must provide clear privacy notices, user consent options, and secure access to personal information.

SOC 2 compliance requires organizations to undergo an independent SOC 2 audit, conducted by an accredited third-party auditor. The audit evaluates the organization's security controls, operational processes, and adherence to the trust service criteria. There are two types of SOC

2 reports: SOC 2 Type I and SOC 2 Type II. SOC 2 Type I evaluates an organization's security controls at a specific point in time, while SOC 2 Type II assesses security controls over an extended period (typically 3 to 12 months). The Type II audit provides a more comprehensive evaluation of how effectively security controls function over time. Organizations that achieve SOC 2 Type II certification demonstrate a strong commitment to ongoing security and compliance.

Cloud security compliance extends beyond SOC 2, requiring organizations to align with global security frameworks such as ISO 27001, NIST 800-53, and FedRAMP. These frameworks provide additional security requirements for risk management, access control, encryption, and incident response. Cloud service providers operating in highly regulated industries must also comply with GDPR, HIPAA, and PCI DSS, ensuring that cloud environments meet data protection and financial security standards. Organizations should conduct third-party security assessments, vulnerability scans, and penetration testing to verify compliance with cloud security regulations.

One of the biggest challenges in cloud security compliance is shared responsibility between cloud providers and customers. Cloud service providers, such as AWS, Microsoft Azure, and Google Cloud, implement security controls to protect cloud infrastructure, but customers are responsible for securing applications, configurations, access controls, and data. Misconfigured cloud environments often lead to data breaches, unauthorized access, and compliance violations. Organizations must implement identity and access management (IAM), least privilege access policies, encryption, and continuous monitoring to maintain security in cloud environments.

Continuous security monitoring, compliance automation, and third-party risk management are essential for maintaining SOC 2 and cloud security compliance. Organizations should deploy cloud security posture management (CSPM) tools, compliance dashboards, and automated security assessments to detect misconfigurations and compliance gaps. Implementing security orchestration, automation, and response (SOAR) solutions enhances incident response and regulatory compliance by automating security workflows and reporting.

Cloud compliance frameworks continue to evolve to address emerging cyber threats, regulatory requirements, and advanced security technologies. Organizations must stay updated with SOC 2 updates, cloud security best practices, and industry regulations to maintain compliance. As cloud computing adoption grows, businesses must integrate zero-trust security models, advanced threat detection, and privacy-enhancing technologies to strengthen their cloud security posture. Achieving SOC 2 compliance and aligning with cloud security frameworks ensures that organizations protect customer data, maintain regulatory compliance, and mitigate cybersecurity risks in an increasingly complex cloud environment.

HIPAA and Healthcare Cybersecurity

The Health Insurance Portability and Accountability Act (HIPAA) is a critical regulation that establishes standards for protecting sensitive patient information within the healthcare industry. Enacted in 1996 by the U.S. government, HIPAA was designed to improve the portability of health insurance and safeguard medical records against unauthorized access and disclosure. With the increasing digitization of healthcare records and the rise of cyber threats targeting medical institutions, HIPAA compliance has become essential for ensuring data security, patient privacy, and regulatory adherence. Healthcare organizations, including hospitals, insurance providers, and third-party service providers, must implement strong cybersecurity controls to prevent data breaches and maintain HIPAA compliance.

HIPAA consists of several key rules that govern how healthcare organizations must handle protected health information (PHI). The Privacy Rule establishes national standards for the protection of PHI, defining who can access patient information, how data should be shared, and what rights patients have over their medical records. This rule ensures that individuals have control over their health information while allowing healthcare providers to exchange data securely for treatment, billing, and operational purposes. Covered entities must provide clear privacy notices, obtain patient consent for data sharing, and establish policies for disclosing PHI.

The Security Rule focuses on safeguarding electronic protected health information (ePHI) by requiring healthcare organizations to implement administrative, technical, and physical security measures. Administrative safeguards include risk assessments, employee training, and incident response plans, ensuring that organizations proactively identify and mitigate security threats. Technical safeguards involve encryption, multi-factor authentication (MFA), intrusion detection systems (IDS), and secure access controls, protecting ePHI from cyberattacks. Physical safeguards require organizations to secure workstations, restrict access to data centers, and implement security measures for mobile devices and backup storage systems.

Another critical component of HIPAA compliance is the Breach Notification Rule, which mandates that organizations notify affected individuals, the U.S. Department of Health and Human Services (HHS), and, in some cases, the media, in the event of a data breach. The notification must occur within 60 days of discovering the breach, detailing the nature of the incident, the affected data, and steps taken to mitigate risks. Healthcare organizations must have an incident response plan to quickly detect, contain, and report breaches while minimizing the impact on patients and operations. Failure to report a breach can result in significant financial penalties and reputational damage.

HIPAA compliance also extends to third-party vendors that process or handle patient data. The Business Associate Agreement (BAA) requires that any third party working with a healthcare entity must comply with HIPAA regulations and implement security measures to protect ePHI. Cloud service providers, billing companies, and IT service providers must sign BAAs before handling sensitive healthcare data. These agreements establish liability, security responsibilities, and contractual obligations to ensure that vendors maintain the same level of security as covered entities.

Cybersecurity threats targeting healthcare organizations have increased in both frequency and sophistication, making HIPAA compliance more important than ever. Ransomware attacks, phishing scams, insider threats, and data breaches are common threats that put patient data at risk. Healthcare institutions are particularly vulnerable because they store highly sensitive information, including medical histories, Social Security numbers, and insurance details, which cybercriminals can exploit for identity theft and financial fraud. A single breach can expose thousands of patient records, leading to financial losses, lawsuits, and damage to an organization's reputation.

Ransomware has emerged as one of the most severe cybersecurity threats in the healthcare industry. Cybercriminals infiltrate healthcare networks, encrypt critical data, and demand ransom payments to restore access. These attacks disrupt hospital operations, delay patient care, and put lives at risk. Under HIPAA, healthcare providers must implement regular data backups, endpoint security measures, and network segmentation to prevent and recover from ransomware attacks. Security teams must also conduct regular penetration testing, vulnerability assessments, and security audits to identify weaknesses before attackers exploit them.

Employee awareness and cybersecurity training are essential for HIPAA compliance and healthcare cybersecurity. Many data breaches occur due to human error, weak passwords, or social engineering attacks. Healthcare employees must be trained to recognize phishing emails, suspicious links, and unauthorized access attempts. Organizations should enforce strong password policies, secure authentication methods, and role-based access control (RBAC) to prevent unauthorized personnel from accessing sensitive information. Regular security awareness programs ensure that employees remain vigilant and adhere to HIPAA security protocols.

Medical devices connected to hospital networks also pose significant cybersecurity risks. The rise of Internet of Medical Things (IoMT) devices, such as smart infusion pumps, remote patient monitoring systems, and connected imaging machines, introduces new attack vectors that cybercriminals can exploit. If compromised, these devices can be used to access patient data, disrupt medical procedures, or even cause harm to patients. To comply with HIPAA, healthcare organizations must implement device security policies, network segmentation, and continuous monitoring to detect and respond to cyber threats targeting medical devices.

HIPAA enforcement is overseen by the Office for Civil Rights (OCR), which investigates complaints and conducts audits to ensure compliance. Organizations found in violation of HIPAA can face significant fines, ranging from $100 to $50,000 per violation, depending on the level of negligence. Severe cases of non-compliance can result in criminal charges and civil lawsuits, making regulatory adherence a top priority for healthcare institutions. To maintain compliance, organizations must conduct regular security risk assessments, document security policies, and establish audit trails for data access and modifications.

Cloud computing has become a key component of modern healthcare infrastructure, allowing organizations to store and share patient data more efficiently. However, cloud environments must meet HIPAA's security and privacy requirements to ensure compliance. Healthcare providers using cloud services must verify that their cloud vendors are HIPAA-compliant, using encryption, secure access controls, and logging mechanisms to protect ePHI. Cloud security frameworks, such as SOC 2 and ISO 27001, can help organizations evaluate the security posture of their cloud providers.

Telemedicine and remote healthcare services have also increased the demand for secure communication channels and encrypted patient data transmission. HIPAA requires that telehealth platforms, video conferencing applications, and electronic health record (EHR) systems implement end-to-end encryption, secure login mechanisms, and HIPAA-compliant storage solutions. Healthcare providers must ensure that remote consultations and patient data exchanges remain protected against unauthorized access and cyber threats.

HIPAA and healthcare cybersecurity continue to evolve as new technologies and threats emerge. Healthcare organizations must stay updated with regulatory changes, security best practices, and evolving cyber risks to maintain compliance and protect patient data. By implementing strong access controls, encryption, employee training, incident response plans, and third-party security agreements, healthcare providers can enhance their cybersecurity posture and ensure compliance with HIPAA's stringent security and privacy requirements.

Security Controls and Risk Mitigation

Security controls and risk mitigation are fundamental components of a strong cybersecurity strategy, enabling organizations to protect their assets, prevent cyber threats, and minimize potential damage from security incidents. Security controls are measures implemented to reduce risks, enforce policies, and safeguard data, systems, and networks from unauthorized access, breaches, and attacks. Risk mitigation involves identifying vulnerabilities, assessing threats, and applying security controls to reduce the likelihood and impact of security breaches. Organizations must adopt a layered security approach to address evolving threats and maintain a resilient cybersecurity posture.

Security controls are categorized into three main types: preventive, detective, and corrective controls. Preventive controls are designed to stop security incidents before they occur. These include access controls, encryption, firewalls, and security policies that restrict unauthorized activities. Detective controls help organizations identify and respond to security threats in real time. These include intrusion detection systems (IDS), security monitoring tools, and audit logs that provide visibility into system activities. Corrective controls focus on minimizing damage and restoring normal operations after a security incident. These include data backups, incident response plans, and system recovery procedures that help organizations recover from cyberattacks.

A key preventive control is identity and access management (IAM), which ensures that only authorized users can access sensitive data and systems. Organizations implement IAM by enforcing strong authentication mechanisms such as multi-factor authentication (MFA), role-based access control (RBAC), and least privilege access policies. MFA requires users to verify their identity using multiple factors, such as passwords, biometrics, or one-time codes, making it more difficult for attackers to gain unauthorized access. RBAC restricts access based on user roles, ensuring that employees can only access the information necessary for their job functions. Least privilege access limits users' permissions to the minimum level required to perform their tasks, reducing the risk of insider threats and unauthorized data exposure.

Encryption is another essential security control used to protect sensitive data from unauthorized access. Organizations encrypt data at rest, in transit, and during processing to ensure confidentiality and prevent interception by cybercriminals. End-to-end encryption (E2EE), Transport Layer Security (TLS), and Advanced Encryption Standard (AES) are commonly used encryption protocols that safeguard data across networks and storage environments. Encryption ensures that even if attackers gain access to data, they cannot read or use it without the appropriate decryption keys.

Network security controls play a crucial role in mitigating risks related to unauthorized access, malware infections, and data breaches. Firewalls are the first line of defense, filtering incoming and outgoing traffic based on predefined security rules. Intrusion prevention systems (IPS) actively block malicious activities, while intrusion detection systems (IDS) monitor network traffic for suspicious behavior. Organizations also deploy virtual private networks (VPNs) to encrypt remote connections and secure data transmissions between users and corporate networks. Implementing zero-trust security models further strengthens network defenses by continuously verifying the identity and security posture of users and devices before granting access.

Security awareness training is an effective preventive control that reduces the risk of human error and social engineering attacks. Many cybersecurity breaches occur due to phishing scams, weak passwords, and accidental data exposure. Organizations conduct regular training sessions, simulated phishing tests, and security awareness campaigns to educate employees on recognizing cyber threats and following security best practices. Employees are trained to identify phishing emails, avoid clicking on suspicious links, and report security incidents promptly. By fostering a culture of cybersecurity awareness, organizations significantly reduce the risk of successful cyberattacks.

Detective security controls provide real-time visibility into security threats, helping organizations detect and respond to attacks before they escalate. Security information and event management (SIEM) systems aggregate and analyze logs from various security tools, identifying patterns that indicate potential security breaches. Endpoint detection and response (EDR) solutions monitor devices for suspicious activities and automatically contain threats. Organizations also use threat intelligence feeds and anomaly detection algorithms to detect emerging cyber threats and vulnerabilities. Continuous security monitoring enables security teams to detect and respond to threats proactively, minimizing the impact of attacks.

Risk mitigation strategies involve regular vulnerability assessments, penetration testing, and security audits to identify weaknesses in security controls and address them before attackers exploit them. Organizations conduct automated vulnerability scans and manual penetration tests to evaluate the security of applications, networks, and infrastructure. Security audits assess compliance with industry standards and regulatory requirements, ensuring that organizations maintain a secure environment. Implementing patch management policies ensures that software and systems are updated regularly to fix security vulnerabilities and reduce the risk of exploitation.

Incident response and disaster recovery planning are essential corrective controls that help organizations minimize damage and restore operations after a security breach. A well-defined incident response plan (IRP) outlines the steps to be taken when a cyber incident occurs, including containment, investigation, eradication, recovery, and post-incident analysis. Organizations conduct tabletop exercises and red team drills to test their incident response capabilities and improve coordination between security teams. Disaster recovery plans (DRPs) ensure that organizations can restore critical systems, recover data, and resume operations after cyberattacks, hardware failures, or natural disasters.

Data backups are an essential corrective control that helps organizations recover from ransomware attacks and accidental data loss. Regular backups ensure that organizations can restore data in the event of a security breach or system failure. Implementing offline, encrypted, and geographically distributed backups protects against ransomware encryption and physical disasters. Organizations follow the 3-2-1 backup rule, which involves maintaining three copies of data on two different storage types, with one copy stored offsite.

Security controls and risk mitigation require continuous improvement to address evolving cyber threats. Organizations adopt security frameworks such as NIST, ISO 27001, and CIS Controls to guide their risk management strategies and implement best practices. Implementing a risk-based approach ensures that security resources are allocated effectively to protect the most critical assets and mitigate high-priority threats. Security teams continuously evaluate emerging threats, update security policies, and enhance security controls to strengthen their cybersecurity resilience.

By integrating preventive, detective, and corrective security controls, organizations reduce their exposure to cyber threats and improve their ability to detect and respond to security incidents. Security awareness, strong access controls, encryption, continuous monitoring, and incident response planning collectively form a comprehensive cybersecurity strategy that minimizes risk and ensures the protection of sensitive data, systems, and business operations.

Identity and Access Management (IAM)

Identity and Access Management (IAM) is a fundamental component of cybersecurity, ensuring that only authorized individuals have access to the right resources at the right time. IAM involves the processes, policies, and technologies that manage user identities, control access to systems, and enforce security measures to prevent unauthorized access. As organizations expand their digital environments, adopt cloud services, and support remote workforces, effective IAM strategies become essential for protecting sensitive data, reducing insider threats, and ensuring compliance with regulatory requirements.

IAM consists of three primary functions: identification, authentication, and authorization. Identification establishes the identity of a user, device, or system attempting to access a resource. Authentication verifies the claimed identity using credentials such as passwords, biometrics, or cryptographic tokens. Authorization determines the level of access granted based on predefined policies, ensuring that users can only access the resources necessary for their role. These functions work together to create a secure and efficient access control system that minimizes security risks while maintaining user productivity.

One of the core principles of IAM is the principle of least privilege (PoLP), which states that users should only be granted the minimum level of access required to perform their job functions. By restricting unnecessary access, organizations reduce the risk of insider threats, accidental data exposure, and privilege escalation attacks. Implementing least privilege requires organizations to continuously review and adjust access rights, ensuring that users do not retain excessive permissions as their roles change. Automated tools, such as identity governance and administration (IGA) solutions, help enforce PoLP by providing visibility into user permissions and flagging excessive access.

Multi-factor authentication (MFA) is a crucial IAM security measure that strengthens authentication by requiring users to verify their identity using multiple factors. MFA typically combines something the user knows (password or PIN), something they have (security token or mobile app), and something they are (biometric data such as fingerprints or facial recognition). By implementing MFA, organizations significantly reduce the risk of account compromises caused by stolen passwords or phishing attacks. Many regulatory frameworks, including GDPR, HIPAA, and PCI DSS, mandate the use of MFA for accessing sensitive systems and data.

Single sign-on (SSO) enhances user experience and security by allowing individuals to authenticate once and gain access to multiple applications and services without re-entering credentials. SSO solutions improve efficiency by reducing password fatigue and minimizing the risk of weak password usage. However, SSO must be implemented securely to prevent attackers from exploiting a compromised SSO session. Organizations often pair SSO with MFA to add an additional layer of security, ensuring that authentication remains robust even if a single credential is compromised.

Role-based access control (RBAC) and attribute-based access control (ABAC) are two commonly used IAM models that define how users gain access to resources. RBAC assigns access permissions based on predefined job roles, simplifying access management and ensuring that users only have permissions relevant to their responsibilities. ABAC takes a more dynamic approach, granting access based on attributes such as user location, device type, and security posture. ABAC allows for more granular and context-aware access decisions, making it ideal for modern, cloud-based environments where access conditions frequently change.

Privileged access management (PAM) is a specialized IAM discipline focused on securing and monitoring accounts with elevated privileges, such as system administrators and database managers. Privileged accounts are high-value targets for cybercriminals, as they provide extensive control over an organization's IT infrastructure. PAM solutions enforce strict access controls, require MFA for privileged access, and monitor administrative activity to detect suspicious behavior. Organizations implement just-in-time (JIT) access models to provide temporary privilege elevation only when necessary, reducing the exposure of privileged credentials.

Identity federation allows users to access multiple systems using a single identity managed by a trusted identity provider. This is particularly useful for organizations using cloud services and third-party applications. Federated identity management leverages standards such as Security Assertion Markup Language (SAML) and OpenID Connect (OIDC) to enable secure authentication across different platforms. Identity federation simplifies access management, reduces password-related security risks, and enhances collaboration between organizations and external partners.

IAM plays a crucial role in securing cloud environments, where traditional perimeter-based security models are no longer sufficient. Cloud IAM solutions integrate with cloud service providers to enforce access controls, monitor user activity, and ensure compliance with security policies. Organizations adopt zero-trust security models, where every access request is continuously verified based on user identity, device security posture, and contextual factors. Cloud IAM solutions provide real-time access monitoring, allowing security teams to detect and respond to unauthorized access attempts.

Regulatory compliance is a major driver for IAM adoption, as many data protection laws and industry standards require strict access controls to protect sensitive information. Regulations such as GDPR, HIPAA, SOX, and ISO 27001 mandate that organizations implement IAM policies to prevent unauthorized data access. Compliance audits often evaluate IAM practices, including access reviews, authentication mechanisms, and identity lifecycle management. Failure to comply with IAM-related regulations can result in significant financial penalties, reputational damage, and security breaches.

Automated identity lifecycle management streamlines IAM processes by provisioning and deprovisioning user access based on role changes, employment status, or security policies. When an employee joins an organization, IAM solutions automatically assign appropriate access based on their job function. If an employee changes roles or leaves the organization, their access rights are adjusted or revoked immediately to prevent unauthorized access. Identity lifecycle management reduces administrative overhead, improves security, and ensures compliance with access control policies.

IAM solutions generate vast amounts of authentication and access logs, which security teams analyze for signs of suspicious activity. Security information and event management (SIEM) platforms aggregate IAM logs to detect anomalies, such as multiple failed login attempts, unusual access locations, or unauthorized privilege escalations. Behavioral analytics and artificial intelligence (AI) enhance IAM security by identifying patterns indicative of credential theft, insider threats, or compromised accounts. Organizations leverage machine learning algorithms to detect deviations from normal user behavior and trigger automated security responses.

Organizations continuously improve their IAM strategies by conducting regular access reviews, penetration testing, and security awareness training. Periodic access reviews help identify inactive accounts, excessive permissions, and potential security gaps. Penetration testing evaluates IAM defenses by simulating real-world attacks on authentication mechanisms and access controls. Employee training ensures that users understand the importance of strong passwords, recognizing phishing attempts, and following security policies to protect their identities.

IAM is an essential cybersecurity discipline that governs how users interact with digital resources while enforcing strict security controls. By implementing strong authentication, access control models, privileged access management, and identity monitoring, organizations can reduce security risks, enhance user experience, and comply with regulatory requirements. As cyber threats continue to evolve, organizations must adopt zero-trust security principles, automation, and AI-driven analytics to strengthen their IAM programs and protect their digital assets from unauthorized access and identity-based attacks.

Zero Trust and Governance

Zero Trust is a modern security framework that assumes no user, device, or system should be trusted by default, regardless of whether it is inside or outside an organization's network. This model shifts away from traditional perimeter-based security, where trust was granted to users and devices within a corporate network. Instead, Zero Trust enforces continuous verification, least privilege access, and strict segmentation to minimize the risk of cyber threats. Governance plays a critical role in Zero Trust by establishing policies, compliance requirements, and oversight mechanisms that ensure security measures align with business objectives and regulatory standards.

The core principle of Zero Trust is "never trust, always verify." Unlike conventional security models that assume networks are secure, Zero Trust requires organizations to authenticate and validate every access request, device connection, and data exchange. This approach prevents lateral movement by attackers who exploit compromised credentials or unprotected network segments. Organizations implementing Zero Trust rely on multiple security controls, including identity and access management (IAM), multi-factor authentication (MFA), least privilege access, micro-segmentation, and continuous monitoring.

Governance within a Zero Trust architecture ensures that security policies are consistently applied across all environments, including on-premises infrastructure, cloud platforms, and remote workforces. Organizations must define clear security policies and access control rules that dictate how users and devices interact with corporate resources. Governance frameworks establish accountability, requiring security teams, IT administrators, and compliance officers to enforce Zero Trust principles. Security policies should specify authentication requirements, access review processes, and data protection measures to prevent unauthorized access and data breaches.

Identity and access management (IAM) is a fundamental component of Zero Trust governance. Organizations must implement strong authentication mechanisms, including passwordless authentication, adaptive access controls, and continuous identity verification. Role-based access control (RBAC) and attribute-based access control (ABAC) ensure that users receive only the permissions necessary for their job functions. Governance policies should mandate regular access reviews, privileged account monitoring, and automated deprovisioning of inactive accounts to minimize security risks.

Zero Trust also relies on least privilege access, which restricts user and system permissions to the minimum necessary level. Organizations should enforce just-in-time (JIT) access models, where elevated privileges are granted temporarily based on specific tasks or approval workflows. This reduces the attack surface and limits the impact of compromised credentials. Governance frameworks must establish policies for privileged access management (PAM), requiring multi-factor authentication (MFA) and session monitoring for administrative users. Security audits and compliance checks ensure that least privilege policies are enforced consistently.

Micro-segmentation is another key component of Zero Trust security. Traditional network security models rely on broad network zones, where once an attacker gains access, they can move laterally to compromise other systems. Micro-segmentation divides networks into isolated security zones, restricting communication between applications, workloads, and users based on predefined security policies. Governance ensures that segmentation policies are properly configured and continuously updated to align with security best practices. Organizations must conduct regular network audits, traffic analysis, and compliance reviews to verify that segmentation policies effectively contain threats.

Data security governance is essential in a Zero Trust environment, as organizations must protect sensitive information from unauthorized access and leaks. Zero Trust enforces data classification, encryption, and access controls to ensure that only authorized users can view or modify sensitive data. Governance frameworks require organizations to establish data protection policies, define acceptable use guidelines, and monitor data access behaviors. Security teams should implement data loss prevention (DLP) solutions, endpoint security controls, and behavioral analytics to detect anomalies and prevent insider threats.

Zero Trust also extends to cloud security governance, as organizations increasingly adopt cloud-based applications and services. Cloud environments introduce unique challenges, including dynamic workloads, shared infrastructure, and third-party integrations. Governance frameworks must define cloud security policies, compliance requirements, and vendor risk management procedures to maintain control over cloud-based assets. Organizations should implement cloud access security brokers (CASBs), secure access service edge (SASE), and continuous cloud security posture management (CSPM) to enforce Zero Trust principles in cloud environments.

Continuous monitoring and analytics play a crucial role in Zero Trust security. Unlike traditional models that rely on periodic security assessments, Zero Trust requires real-time monitoring, anomaly detection, and automated threat response. Security information and event management (SIEM) solutions collect and analyze security logs from various sources, identifying suspicious activities and potential breaches. Governance policies should mandate the use of behavioral analytics, machine learning algorithms, and automated incident response playbooks to detect and mitigate threats before they escalate.

Zero Trust governance also involves compliance management, ensuring that organizations adhere to regulatory requirements and industry standards. Many regulations, including GDPR, HIPAA, PCI DSS, and NIST 800-53, require organizations to implement strict access controls, data protection measures, and security monitoring. Governance frameworks establish processes for compliance audits, risk assessments, and security documentation to demonstrate adherence to regulatory requirements. Security teams must work closely with compliance officers and legal departments to ensure that Zero Trust policies align with both business goals and regulatory obligations.

Third-party risk management is another critical aspect of Zero Trust governance. Organizations often rely on external vendors, contractors, and cloud service providers, introducing additional security risks. Governance policies should require third parties to comply with Zero Trust security controls, undergo security assessments, and adhere to contractual security obligations. Organizations should implement zero-trust network access (ZTNA) solutions, which enforce granular access controls for external users and devices, reducing the risk of supply chain attacks.

Adopting Zero Trust requires a cultural shift and executive support. Organizations must establish cybersecurity awareness programs, executive training sessions, and Zero Trust adoption roadmaps to ensure successful implementation. Governance frameworks should include metrics and key performance indicators (KPIs) to measure the effectiveness of Zero Trust initiatives. These metrics may include access control violations, privileged access activity, anomaly detection rates, and incident response times. Continuous evaluation and adaptation are necessary to refine Zero Trust policies and enhance security resilience.

Zero Trust governance is an ongoing process that requires regular security assessments, policy updates, and risk management improvements. Organizations must remain proactive in adapting to new threats, integrating advanced security technologies, and aligning security strategies with evolving business needs. By implementing strong governance frameworks, enforcing least privilege access, and continuously monitoring security events, organizations can strengthen their cybersecurity defenses, reduce the risk of data breaches, and maintain compliance with regulatory standards in an increasingly complex digital environment.

Secure Software Development Governance

Secure software development governance is a critical aspect of cybersecurity that ensures security is integrated throughout the software development lifecycle (SDLC). Organizations must establish policies, frameworks, and best practices to prevent vulnerabilities, mitigate risks, and ensure compliance with security standards. Governance provides oversight and accountability, ensuring that security is not an afterthought but an essential component of software development. With the increasing complexity of software applications and the rise of cyber threats, secure development governance helps organizations build resilient, secure, and compliant software solutions.

Governance in secure software development begins with defining clear security policies and guidelines that align with industry standards and regulatory requirements. Organizations must adopt frameworks such as the Secure Software Development Framework (SSDF), NIST 800-218, OWASP Software Assurance Maturity Model (SAMM), and ISO/IEC 27034 to establish structured security practices. These frameworks provide guidelines for integrating security into development processes, ensuring that software is designed, developed, and tested with security in mind. Governance policies should define security responsibilities for developers, security teams, quality assurance (QA) professionals, and management to ensure a collaborative approach to secure coding.

A fundamental principle of secure software development governance is shift-left security, which emphasizes integrating security early in the development lifecycle rather than treating it as a final step before deployment. Traditional development models often leave security testing for the later stages, increasing the cost and complexity of fixing vulnerabilities. By shifting security left, organizations incorporate security practices in the planning, design, coding, and testing phases of development. Governance ensures that security requirements are included in software specifications, threat modeling is conducted during the design phase, and secure coding practices are followed throughout development.

Threat modeling is a key component of governance that helps identify potential security risks before software is built. Developers and security teams must analyze system architectures, data flows, and attack surfaces to predict possible vulnerabilities and threats. Threat modeling methodologies such as STRIDE (Spoofing, Tampering, Repudiation, Information Disclosure, Denial of Service, Elevation of Privilege) and PASTA (Process for Attack Simulation and Threat Analysis) provide structured approaches to assessing security risks. Governance mandates that threat modeling be an ongoing process, updated as software evolves to address emerging threats and vulnerabilities.

Secure coding practices are essential for reducing software vulnerabilities and ensuring compliance with security policies. Governance frameworks require developers to follow secure coding guidelines such as OWASP Secure Coding Practices, CERT Secure Coding Standards, and Microsoft Secure Coding Guidelines. These guidelines help prevent common vulnerabilities such as SQL injection, cross-site scripting (XSS), buffer overflows, and insecure authentication mechanisms. Organizations should implement static application security testing (SAST) tools to scan source code for security flaws and enforce secure coding policies.

Software composition analysis (SCA) is another critical aspect of secure software development governance. Modern applications rely on third-party libraries, open-source components, and external dependencies that introduce potential security risks. Governance policies must mandate regular SCA scans to detect vulnerabilities in third-party components, ensure compliance with licensing requirements, and mitigate risks associated with outdated or insecure libraries. Vulnerability databases such as the National Vulnerability Database (NVD) and Common Vulnerabilities and Exposures (CVE) repository provide critical information about security flaws in open-source and commercial software components.

Secure development governance also involves dynamic application security testing (DAST) and interactive application security testing (IAST). DAST tools test running applications for vulnerabilities by simulating real-world attacks, helping organizations identify weaknesses in web applications, APIs, and cloud services. IAST combines static and dynamic analysis to provide deeper insights into application security risks. Governance frameworks should establish policies that require automated security testing at multiple stages of development, ensuring that vulnerabilities are detected and remediated before software is deployed.

Organizations adopting DevSecOps integrate security into their continuous integration and continuous deployment (CI/CD) pipelines. Governance ensures that security checks, automated testing, and vulnerability scans are embedded into CI/CD workflows, preventing insecure code from reaching production. Container security policies, infrastructure-as-code (IaC) security scans, and runtime protection mechanisms must be enforced to secure cloud-native applications. Governance frameworks should define policies for secure deployment, access controls, and monitoring in cloud environments to mitigate risks associated with cloud-based software development.

Incident response and vulnerability management play a crucial role in secure software development governance. Organizations must establish vulnerability disclosure programs (VDPs) and bug bounty programs to encourage ethical hacking and responsible vulnerability reporting. Security governance requires developers to adhere to patch management policies, security updates, and rapid incident response procedures when vulnerabilities are discovered. Organizations must track vulnerabilities using Common Weakness Enumeration (CWE) and MITRE ATT&CK frameworks to analyze security trends and improve defenses against software-based attacks.

Regulatory compliance is a key driver for secure software development governance. Many industries must comply with GDPR, HIPAA, PCI DSS, SOC 2, and ISO 27001, which mandate secure coding practices, data protection measures, and security audits. Governance ensures that software meets compliance requirements by implementing security documentation, audit trails, access controls, and encryption policies. Organizations must conduct regular security assessments, penetration testing, and code reviews to validate compliance with regulatory standards.

Security awareness training is a vital component of governance, ensuring that developers understand cybersecurity risks and best practices. Organizations must provide secure coding training, phishing awareness programs, and security certification courses to educate developers on emerging threats and secure software development techniques. Governance mandates that security training be an ongoing effort, with simulated security exercises, red team/blue team drills, and real-world attack scenario testing to improve the security skills of development teams.

Post-deployment security governance ensures that applications remain secure after release. Organizations must implement continuous security monitoring, runtime application self-protection (RASP), and application-layer threat detection to detect and mitigate post-deployment vulnerabilities. Log analysis, anomaly detection, and behavioral analytics help identify potential security incidents and prevent exploits targeting production systems. Governance frameworks must require regular security audits, compliance checks, and software updates to maintain a secure application environment.

Secure software development governance is an ongoing process that requires collaboration between security teams, developers, compliance officers, and business leaders. Organizations must continuously evaluate security policies, refine development practices, and integrate security automation to adapt to evolving cyber threats. By enforcing secure coding guidelines, threat modeling, security testing, and regulatory compliance, organizations can build software that is not only functional and efficient but also resilient against cyber threats and aligned with security best practices.

Cybersecurity Risk Metrics and KPIs

Cybersecurity risk metrics and key performance indicators (KPIs) are essential for measuring the effectiveness of an organization's security program. They provide visibility into security performance, help identify weaknesses, and support data-driven decision-making. Without clear metrics, organizations struggle to assess their cybersecurity posture, making it difficult to allocate resources effectively and mitigate security risks. By defining and tracking the right cybersecurity metrics and KPIs, organizations can evaluate their risk exposure, improve incident response, and ensure compliance with security standards and regulatory requirements.

Cybersecurity metrics provide quantifiable data that help organizations understand their risk landscape. They measure factors such as the number of security incidents, threat detection rates, vulnerability remediation times, and compliance adherence. Metrics serve as indicators of security effectiveness, revealing whether an organization's defenses are improving or if additional measures are needed. KPIs, on the other hand, are specific performance indicators that align security efforts with business objectives. Well-defined KPIs help organizations track progress, optimize security investments, and communicate cybersecurity risks to executive leadership and stakeholders.

One of the most critical cybersecurity risk metrics is the mean time to detect (MTTD), which measures the average time taken to identify a security incident. A lower MTTD indicates that an organization's monitoring and threat detection capabilities are effective. Security teams use security information and event management (SIEM) systems, endpoint detection and response (EDR) tools, and threat intelligence platforms to reduce detection times and improve incident response. Organizations must continuously optimize their detection processes to minimize the time attackers remain undetected within the network.

Closely related to MTTD is the mean time to respond (MTTR), which measures how quickly an organization can contain and mitigate a security incident after detection. A faster MTTR reduces the impact of cyber threats, preventing data breaches, system downtime, and financial losses. Security operations centers (SOCs) track MTTR to evaluate the efficiency of incident response teams. Automated response mechanisms, playbooks, and well-defined incident response plans (IRPs) help security teams accelerate response times and minimize disruptions caused by cyber incidents.

The number of detected security incidents is another key metric that provides insight into an organization's threat landscape. Organizations track incidents such as malware infections, phishing attempts, unauthorized access attempts, and insider threats. An increasing number of security incidents may indicate a growing attack surface or evolving threat tactics. However, it may also suggest that detection mechanisms have improved, allowing security teams to identify more threats before they escalate. Analyzing incident trends helps organizations refine their cybersecurity strategies and enhance preventive measures.

Vulnerability management metrics are crucial for evaluating an organization's ability to detect and remediate security weaknesses. The mean time to remediate (MTTR) vulnerabilities measures how long it takes to fix identified vulnerabilities after discovery. Organizations must prioritize critical vulnerabilities and apply security patches promptly to reduce the risk of exploitation. Patch management KPIs, vulnerability scan frequency, and compliance with patching policies provide additional insight into an organization's security hygiene. Delayed vulnerability remediation increases the likelihood of successful cyberattacks, making timely patching a critical risk mitigation strategy.

The percentage of endpoints with outdated software or missing patches is another important security metric. Organizations must ensure that all devices, including workstations, servers, and IoT devices, remain up to date with the latest security patches. Automated patch management solutions and asset inventory tracking help organizations maintain visibility into system vulnerabilities and enforce security compliance across all endpoints. Monitoring patching effectiveness reduces exposure to known exploits and enhances overall security resilience.

Phishing remains one of the most common attack vectors, making phishing detection and response metrics essential for evaluating cybersecurity awareness and training programs. Organizations track the percentage of employees who report phishing attempts, the click rate on simulated phishing emails, and the success rate of phishing awareness training. A high click rate on phishing emails indicates a need for enhanced training and awareness campaigns. Organizations conduct regular phishing simulations to measure employee resilience against social engineering attacks and improve overall security awareness.

Access management metrics help organizations assess the effectiveness of identity and access management (IAM) controls. The number of failed login attempts, the percentage of accounts with multi-factor authentication (MFA) enabled, and the number of privileged access misuse incidents provide insights into access control security. Organizations monitor user authentication trends to detect brute force attacks, credential stuffing attempts, and unauthorized access activities. Strong IAM policies and continuous authentication monitoring reduce the risk of compromised credentials leading to security breaches.

Compliance-related security metrics ensure that organizations adhere to regulatory requirements such as GDPR, HIPAA, PCI DSS, and ISO 27001. Organizations track compliance audit success rates, the number of security policy violations, and adherence to security training requirements. Security teams conduct regular audits to assess compliance gaps, enforce security policies, and address non-compliant behaviors. Maintaining high compliance scores minimizes legal risks, regulatory fines, and reputational damage associated with security breaches.

Data protection metrics measure an organization's ability to prevent data leaks and unauthorized access to sensitive information. The number of data loss prevention (DLP) incidents, the percentage of encrypted sensitive data, and the number of unauthorized data access attempts help security teams evaluate data security effectiveness. Organizations implement DLP solutions, encryption policies, and access controls to prevent data exfiltration, insider threats, and accidental data exposure. Monitoring data security metrics ensures that sensitive information remains protected from unauthorized access.

Security awareness training effectiveness is another key area for cybersecurity metrics. Organizations track the percentage of employees who complete security training programs, the improvement in security quiz scores, and the reduction in security policy violations over time. A well-trained workforce significantly reduces security risks, as employees become more aware of phishing attacks, social engineering tactics, and secure data handling practices. Organizations implement gamified security training, periodic refresher courses, and role-specific security education to enhance employee engagement and improve cybersecurity awareness.

Network security metrics provide insights into traffic anomalies, intrusion attempts, and firewall effectiveness. Organizations track the number of blocked malicious connections, the percentage of encrypted network traffic, and the rate of false positives in security alerts. Effective network monitoring helps security teams detect denial-of-service (DDoS) attacks, malware propagation, and insider threats. Organizations leverage network traffic analysis, intrusion prevention systems (IPS), and anomaly detection algorithms to enhance network security visibility.

Cybersecurity risk metrics and KPIs play a vital role in measuring security effectiveness, identifying areas for improvement, and demonstrating security posture to stakeholders. By continuously monitoring key security metrics, organizations can refine their cybersecurity strategies, allocate resources effectively, and respond proactively to emerging threats. Security teams must define clear benchmarking standards, automate security analytics, and establish continuous reporting mechanisms to ensure that cybersecurity risk metrics drive informed decision-making and improve overall security resilience.

Continuous Monitoring and Incident Detection

Continuous monitoring and incident detection are critical components of modern cybersecurity strategies, enabling organizations to proactively identify threats, respond to incidents, and reduce security risks. As cyber threats evolve, organizations must implement real-time monitoring mechanisms to detect suspicious activities and prevent security breaches. Continuous monitoring involves the ongoing collection, analysis, and evaluation of security data across networks, endpoints, applications, and cloud environments. By implementing a structured monitoring approach, organizations enhance their ability to detect anomalies, prevent cyberattacks, and maintain compliance with security standards and regulatory requirements.

Incident detection refers to the process of identifying security events that indicate potential threats or ongoing attacks. Organizations rely on Security Information and Event Management (SIEM) systems, intrusion detection systems (IDS), endpoint detection and response (EDR) solutions, and artificial intelligence-driven security analytics to detect incidents in real time. The goal is to identify malicious behavior, unauthorized access attempts, malware infections, insider threats, and compliance violations before they escalate into full-scale breaches. Advanced monitoring techniques help security teams recognize indicators of compromise (IoCs) and respond swiftly to mitigate risks.

A fundamental aspect of continuous monitoring is log management and analysis, which involves collecting and reviewing system logs from various sources, including firewalls, authentication servers, databases, and network devices. SIEM platforms aggregate and correlate log data to detect patterns that may indicate a security threat. Automated threat detection algorithms, machine learning models, and behavioral analytics enhance monitoring capabilities by identifying anomalies that deviate from normal behavior. By analyzing large volumes of security data, organizations can uncover stealthy attacks, advanced persistent threats (APTs), and zero-day exploits that traditional security tools might miss.

Network monitoring plays a crucial role in continuous security surveillance. Organizations deploy network traffic analysis (NTA) tools, deep packet inspection (DPI), and intrusion prevention systems (IPS) to monitor incoming and outgoing data flows. Network-based monitoring detects unauthorized access attempts, lateral movement by attackers, data exfiltration, and command-and-control (C2) communications used by malware. Organizations establish baseline network behavior profiles to distinguish normal activity from potential threats. Any deviation from expected patterns triggers an alert, prompting security teams to investigate potential security incidents.

Endpoint security monitoring is essential for detecting cyber threats on individual devices, including desktops, laptops, mobile devices, and servers. EDR solutions provide real-time endpoint visibility, automated threat detection, and forensic investigation capabilities. Organizations implement host-based intrusion detection systems (HIDS), anti-malware solutions, and memory integrity monitoring to protect endpoints from exploitation. Continuous monitoring ensures that endpoints remain compliant with security policies and do not introduce vulnerabilities into the network.

User behavior analytics (UBA) enhances incident detection by identifying suspicious user activity, credential misuse, and privilege escalation attempts. UBA solutions analyze login patterns, access behavior, and data transfer activities to detect anomalies that may indicate compromised accounts or insider threats. For example, an employee accessing sensitive files outside of normal working hours or from an unfamiliar location may trigger a security alert. Organizations integrate adaptive authentication and risk-based access control to respond dynamically to anomalous user behavior, preventing unauthorized data access and reducing security risks.

Cloud security monitoring is becoming increasingly important as organizations adopt cloud computing and hybrid environments. Traditional perimeter-based security models are insufficient for protecting cloud workloads, making cloud-native security tools, cloud access security brokers (CASBs), and cloud workload protection platforms (CWPPs) essential for continuous monitoring. Organizations must monitor cloud API activity, misconfigured storage permissions, unauthorized account access, and abnormal cloud resource usage to detect and mitigate cloud-specific threats. Security teams enforce zero-trust security models and micro-segmentation to limit exposure to cloud-based attacks.

Incident detection also requires threat intelligence integration, allowing organizations to leverage real-time threat feeds, attack signatures, and known indicators of compromise. Threat intelligence platforms (TIPs) aggregate data from multiple sources, including government agencies, cybersecurity vendors, and open-source communities. Security teams use automated threat intelligence feeds to identify emerging threats, correlate attack patterns, and enhance situational awareness. By integrating threat intelligence with SIEM, organizations improve their ability to detect and respond to cyber threats before they cause significant damage.

Automated response mechanisms are critical for reducing incident response times and minimizing the impact of cyber threats. Security orchestration, automation, and response (SOAR) platforms help organizations automate threat containment, trigger remediation workflows, and enforce security policies dynamically. Automated playbooks enable security teams to block malicious IP addresses, isolate infected endpoints, disable compromised accounts, and notify stakeholders when an incident is detected. Automating routine security tasks allows security analysts to focus on complex threat investigations and incident resolution.

Continuous monitoring must extend to third-party and supply chain risk management, as organizations increasingly rely on external vendors, cloud service providers, and contractors. Vendor security assessments, third-party access monitoring, and continuous compliance checks ensure that external entities adhere to security policies and best practices. Organizations implement least privilege access controls, secure remote access solutions, and continuous security validation to prevent third-party security breaches. Monitoring third-party activity helps detect supply chain attacks, unauthorized data access, and policy violations that could compromise security.

Regulatory compliance plays a key role in continuous monitoring, as many industries must adhere to security standards such as GDPR, HIPAA, PCI DSS, NIST 800-53, and ISO 27001. Compliance-driven monitoring involves real-time security audits, automated compliance reporting, and continuous control assessments to ensure adherence to regulatory requirements. Organizations use compliance dashboards and audit logs to track security performance, identify gaps, and demonstrate compliance to auditors and regulators. Continuous compliance monitoring reduces legal risks and strengthens an organization's cybersecurity posture.

Organizations must establish incident detection and escalation protocols to ensure that security teams respond effectively to threats. Well-defined incident response workflows, security event categorization, and escalation procedures help organizations prioritize and address incidents based on severity. Security operations centers (SOCs) conduct incident response drills, red team exercises, and penetration testing to evaluate detection capabilities and improve response times. Real-world attack simulations enhance readiness and ensure that security teams are equipped to handle cyber threats efficiently.

Cybersecurity awareness training and continuous education programs support effective monitoring and incident detection. Employees must be trained to recognize security threats, report suspicious activities, and follow security policies. Phishing simulations, role-based security training, and insider threat awareness programs improve an organization's security culture. A well-trained workforce serves as an additional layer of defense against cyber threats, complementing automated monitoring tools and security technologies.

Continuous monitoring and incident detection require a proactive, multi-layered approach to cybersecurity. Organizations must integrate real-time analytics, automation, threat intelligence, and adaptive security controls to detect and mitigate threats before they escalate. By maintaining continuous visibility across networks, endpoints, cloud environments, and user activities, organizations enhance their ability to prevent breaches, respond to incidents, and ensure compliance with cybersecurity regulations.

Security Incident Response and Governance

Security incident response and governance are essential components of a comprehensive cybersecurity strategy. As cyber threats continue to evolve, organizations must establish structured processes to detect, analyze, contain, and recover from security incidents. Incident response is the structured approach used to manage and mitigate cyber incidents, while governance ensures that these processes align with organizational policies, regulatory requirements, and industry best practices. A well-defined incident response framework enables organizations to respond to cyber threats effectively, reducing the impact of security breaches and maintaining business continuity.

Governance in incident response involves establishing policies, assigning roles and responsibilities, defining escalation procedures, and ensuring compliance with security standards. Organizations must implement an Incident Response Plan (IRP) that outlines the steps to be taken when a security breach occurs. This plan serves as a blueprint for security teams, ensuring a coordinated and consistent response to incidents such as malware infections, data breaches, insider threats, and denial-of-service attacks. Governance frameworks provide oversight, ensuring that incident response procedures align with regulatory requirements such as GDPR, HIPAA, PCI DSS, and NIST 800-61.

The incident response lifecycle consists of several key phases: preparation, detection, analysis, containment, eradication, recovery, and post-incident review. Each phase is critical to ensuring that security teams respond efficiently and minimize damage. Governance ensures that these phases are followed consistently, security policies are enforced, and continuous improvements are made based on lessons learned from previous incidents.

The preparation phase is essential for ensuring that organizations are ready to handle security incidents before they occur. This involves developing incident response policies, creating playbooks, training security teams, and conducting tabletop exercises to simulate cyberattacks. Organizations must also establish an incident response team (IRT) composed of security analysts, IT personnel, legal advisors, and compliance officers. Governance ensures that incident response policies are regularly reviewed and updated to address emerging threats and evolving regulatory requirements.

Detection and analysis are critical for identifying security incidents in real time. Organizations use Security Information and Event Management (SIEM) systems, intrusion detection systems (IDS), endpoint detection and response (EDR) tools, and behavioral analytics to monitor for suspicious activity. Incident response governance mandates the implementation of automated alerts, anomaly detection, and log analysis to identify threats as early as possible. Security teams analyze incidents based on predefined severity levels, ensuring that high-risk incidents are escalated and addressed promptly.

Once a security incident is detected, the containment phase focuses on preventing the threat from spreading. Governance frameworks define containment strategies based on incident severity, system impact, and business continuity requirements. Organizations implement network segmentation, access revocation, malware quarantine, and firewall rule modifications to isolate affected systems. The containment strategy must be well-documented and tested regularly to ensure its effectiveness during real-world incidents.

The eradication phase involves eliminating the root cause of the incident and ensuring that affected systems are free of malicious artifacts. Security teams perform forensic investigations, threat intelligence analysis, and system hardening to remove threats and close security gaps. Governance ensures that eradication procedures follow documented best practices, forensic evidence handling guidelines, and compliance requirements to maintain legal and regulatory integrity. Security teams must validate that no backdoors, persistent threats, or unauthorized access points remain in the system.

During the recovery phase, organizations restore affected systems, services, and operations to normal functionality. This involves patching vulnerabilities, reconfiguring security controls, restoring data from backups, and validating system integrity. Governance ensures that recovery procedures follow business continuity and disaster recovery (BC/DR) plans, minimizing downtime and operational disruptions. Security teams must conduct post-recovery validation tests, system monitoring, and risk assessments to confirm that threats have been fully eradicated before resuming normal operations.

The post-incident review phase focuses on analyzing the incident, identifying lessons learned, and implementing security improvements. Governance mandates that organizations document the incident, evaluate response effectiveness, and refine incident response strategies. Security teams must update security policies, enhance monitoring capabilities, and improve employee training programs based on insights gained from the incident. Incident response governance requires organizations to maintain comprehensive incident reports, regulatory compliance records, and audit logs to demonstrate accountability and continuous improvement.

Incident response governance also includes regulatory compliance and legal considerations. Organizations must adhere to breach notification laws, data protection regulations, and industry security standards when handling security incidents. GDPR, for example, requires organizations to report data breaches within 72 hours, while HIPAA mandates breach notifications for healthcare-related incidents. Governance ensures that legal teams, compliance officers, and data protection officers (DPOs) are involved in the incident response process to manage legal risks and regulatory reporting requirements.

Security teams must also focus on threat intelligence sharing to enhance incident response capabilities. Governance frameworks encourage organizations to participate in cyber threat intelligence (CTI) programs, industry-specific information sharing and analysis centers (ISACs), and government-led cybersecurity initiatives. By sharing and receiving threat intelligence, organizations can proactively defend against known attack vectors, improve threat detection capabilities, and enhance situational awareness.

Automated security orchestration, automation, and response (SOAR) solutions improve the efficiency of incident response by automating repetitive tasks, coordinating remediation efforts, and enforcing security policies. Governance ensures that SOAR platforms align with incident response playbooks, enabling security teams to automatically block malicious IP addresses, revoke compromised credentials, and isolate infected endpoints based on predefined security rules. Automation reduces response times and allows security analysts to focus on complex threat investigations.

Organizations must also implement security awareness training to ensure that employees understand their role in incident detection and response. Governance mandates regular phishing simulations, role-based security training, and incident response drills to enhance employee preparedness. A well-informed workforce reduces the likelihood of human error, improves threat reporting, and strengthens the overall cybersecurity posture.

Effective security incident response and governance require continuous improvement, regular security assessments, and proactive threat hunting. Organizations conduct red team exercises, penetration testing, and security audits to evaluate the effectiveness of their incident response strategies. Governance frameworks ensure that security teams review performance metrics, update response procedures, and adapt to evolving cyber threats.

By implementing structured incident response processes, enforcing governance policies, and leveraging advanced security technologies, organizations can detect, contain, and recover from cyber incidents more effectively. Governance provides the necessary oversight to ensure that incident response aligns with regulatory compliance, industry best practices, and business objectives, reducing the overall impact of security incidents and strengthening an organization's resilience against cyber threats.

Cyber Resilience and Business Continuity

Cyber resilience and business continuity are critical components of an organization's overall security strategy. Cyber resilience refers to an organization's ability to prepare for, respond to, and recover from cyber threats while maintaining essential business operations. It extends beyond traditional cybersecurity by integrating risk management, incident response, disaster recovery, and governance into a comprehensive approach to ensuring business continuity. Organizations must adopt a proactive and adaptive mindset to mitigate the impact of cyber incidents and maintain operational stability in the face of evolving threats.

Business continuity focuses on ensuring that critical business functions remain operational despite disruptions caused by cyberattacks, natural disasters, hardware failures, or human errors. A business continuity plan (BCP) outlines the strategies and procedures that organizations must follow to minimize downtime, protect data, and restore services after an incident. Cyber resilience enhances business continuity by incorporating security measures that prevent disruptions and enable rapid recovery from cyber threats such as ransomware, data breaches, denial-of-service attacks, and insider threats.

A fundamental aspect of cyber resilience is risk assessment and management, which involves identifying potential threats, evaluating vulnerabilities, and implementing mitigation strategies. Organizations must conduct cyber risk assessments, threat modeling, and impact analysis to determine the likelihood and potential consequences of cyber incidents. Governance frameworks, such as NIST Cybersecurity Framework, ISO 27001, and CIS Controls, provide structured methodologies for assessing and managing cyber risks. Security teams prioritize risks based on their potential impact and implement preventive controls, detection mechanisms, and incident response plans to mitigate threats.

Cyber resilience also relies on redundancy and failover mechanisms to ensure that business operations can continue during a cyber incident. Organizations implement backup systems, redundant network connections, and alternative processing sites to maintain functionality in case of system failures or cyberattacks. Cloud-based disaster recovery solutions provide scalable and flexible options for ensuring data availability and system resilience. Automated failover systems, load balancing, and real-time data replication enable seamless transitions to backup systems, minimizing operational disruptions.

Incident response and crisis management play a crucial role in cyber resilience by ensuring that organizations can react quickly and effectively to security incidents. Organizations must develop and regularly update incident response plans (IRPs) and crisis communication strategies to coordinate response efforts and mitigate damage. Security teams conduct tabletop exercises, penetration testing, and red team assessments to validate response capabilities and improve coordination between departments. Effective incident handling, containment strategies, and forensic investigations help organizations recover from cyber incidents and prevent future attacks.

Cyber resilience requires continuous monitoring and threat intelligence to detect and respond to cyber threats in real time. Organizations deploy security information and event management (SIEM) systems, intrusion detection systems (IDS), endpoint detection and response (EDR) solutions, and behavioral analytics to monitor security events and identify anomalies. Threat intelligence feeds, security analytics, and machine learning algorithms enhance detection capabilities, enabling organizations to respond to cyber threats proactively. Security teams use real-time alerts, automated incident response workflows, and threat hunting techniques to strengthen cyber resilience and prevent operational disruptions.

Data protection and secure backup strategies are essential components of business continuity planning. Organizations must implement regular data backups, encryption, and secure storage solutions to protect critical business data from cyber threats. The 3-2-1 backup strategy ensures data redundancy by maintaining three copies of data on two different storage media, with one copy stored offsite. Organizations must conduct backup integrity testing, disaster recovery simulations, and secure cloud storage implementations to ensure data availability and reliability. Immutable backups, air-gapped storage, and ransomware-resistant backup solutions further enhance data resilience against cyber threats.

Cyber resilience and business continuity require strong access controls and identity management to prevent unauthorized access and insider threats. Organizations implement multi-factor authentication (MFA), role-based access control (RBAC), and privileged access management (PAM) to enforce strict security policies. Zero-trust security models and continuous authentication mechanisms further enhance cyber resilience by verifying user identities, device integrity, and access permissions before granting access to critical systems. Identity and access management (IAM) solutions enable organizations to monitor user activities, detect anomalous behavior, and enforce security policies across distributed environments.

Regulatory compliance and governance frameworks ensure that cyber resilience strategies align with legal requirements, industry standards, and best practices. Many regulations, including GDPR, HIPAA, PCI DSS, NIST 800-53, and ISO 22301, mandate organizations to implement business continuity measures and cybersecurity controls. Compliance audits, security assessments, and regulatory reporting help organizations demonstrate adherence to security and resilience requirements. Governance frameworks establish accountability, risk ownership, and policy enforcement mechanisms to ensure that cyber resilience remains a priority at all levels of the organization.

Employee awareness and training programs are essential for maintaining cyber resilience and business continuity. Organizations must conduct regular security awareness training, phishing simulations, and incident response drills to educate employees on security best practices. A culture of cybersecurity awareness ensures that employees recognize and respond to potential threats, reducing the likelihood of successful cyberattacks. Security teams develop role-based training programs, executive-level cyber resilience workshops, and insider threat awareness campaigns to strengthen security awareness across the organization.

Cloud computing and digital transformation initiatives introduce new challenges for cyber resilience and business continuity. Organizations must adopt cloud security best practices, secure DevOps methodologies, and cloud-native security controls to maintain resilience in cloud environments. Multi-cloud security strategies, hybrid cloud resilience planning, and secure cloud workload protection (CWP) help organizations mitigate cloud-specific risks. Cloud security governance frameworks, such as CSA STAR and SOC 2, provide guidance on ensuring security, compliance, and operational resilience in cloud-based environments.

Cyber resilience and business continuity must be continuously tested, refined, and improved to adapt to emerging threats and evolving business requirements. Organizations conduct regular disaster recovery tests, cyber crisis simulations, and business impact analyses to validate resilience strategies. Security teams use key performance indicators (KPIs) and risk metrics to measure cyber resilience effectiveness, track incident response efficiency, and improve business continuity planning. Automated security assessments, real-time monitoring, and continuous security validation enable organizations to enhance resilience against cyber threats and ensure operational continuity.

By integrating cyber resilience and business continuity planning, organizations can protect critical assets, maintain regulatory compliance, and sustain operations in the face of cyber incidents. Strong governance, continuous monitoring, incident response preparedness, and employee training contribute to a resilient security posture. Organizations that prioritize cyber resilience are better equipped to withstand cyber threats, recover from disruptions, and maintain long-term business stability in an increasingly complex cybersecurity landscape.

Internal Audits and Cybersecurity Oversight

Internal audits and cybersecurity oversight are critical components of an organization's security governance framework. They provide a structured approach to evaluating cybersecurity controls, identifying vulnerabilities, and ensuring compliance with regulatory requirements and industry standards. By conducting regular internal audits, organizations can assess the effectiveness of their security policies, detect weaknesses before they are exploited, and implement corrective measures to strengthen their cybersecurity posture. Cybersecurity oversight ensures that security risks are continuously monitored, managed, and aligned with business objectives, regulatory mandates, and industry best practices.

Internal audits play a vital role in validating an organization's security controls and risk management strategies. Auditors review access controls, network security configurations, incident response plans, vulnerability management practices, and compliance adherence to determine whether security measures are functioning as intended. These audits follow a structured methodology that includes risk assessments, evidence collection, control testing, and reporting to provide executive leadership with insights into cybersecurity effectiveness. Internal audits help organizations identify gaps in security policies, misconfigurations, and emerging risks that could impact business operations.

A well-defined cybersecurity audit program consists of several key phases: planning, execution, analysis, reporting, and follow-up. During the planning phase, organizations define the audit scope, objectives, and key risk areas to assess. The execution phase involves gathering security logs, reviewing access controls, interviewing security personnel, and testing security controls. Analysis includes evaluating audit findings, assessing control effectiveness, and identifying areas for improvement. The reporting phase documents audit results, including identified risks, non-compliance issues, and recommended corrective actions. Follow-up activities ensure that remediation efforts are implemented and validated to address security weaknesses.

Cybersecurity audits assess an organization's adherence to security frameworks such as NIST Cybersecurity Framework, ISO 27001, CIS Controls, and COBIT. These frameworks provide guidelines for implementing robust security controls, managing risk, and ensuring continuous security improvement. Internal audits also help organizations prepare for external regulatory audits, industry certifications, and third-party security assessments, ensuring that security measures meet compliance requirements for regulations such as GDPR, HIPAA, PCI DSS, and SOX.

One critical aspect of cybersecurity oversight is continuous monitoring and real-time risk assessment. Security teams use Security Information and Event Management (SIEM) systems, automated compliance tools, and threat intelligence platforms to track security metrics, detect anomalies, and analyze potential threats. Continuous oversight allows organizations to adapt their security strategies based on evolving cyber threats, regulatory changes, and industry developments. Organizations conduct risk-based audits that prioritize high-risk areas, such as privileged access management, cloud security, third-party risk management, and data protection.

Cybersecurity governance ensures that security oversight is integrated into the organization's executive leadership, board-level discussions, and strategic decision-making. The role of Chief Information Security Officers (CISOs), risk committees, and security advisory boards is to oversee security policies, manage cyber risks, and align security efforts with business goals. Governance frameworks require organizations to define cybersecurity roles and responsibilities, ensuring that security teams, IT departments, compliance officers, and risk management personnel collaborate to maintain a secure environment.

Risk-based auditing approaches allow organizations to allocate resources effectively by focusing on the most critical security risks. Cybersecurity auditors evaluate access logs, privileged account activity, network traffic anomalies, and data protection controls to assess potential security threats. Automated security assessments and penetration testing help validate whether security defenses are effective against real-world attack scenarios. Organizations use red team/blue team exercises, breach simulations, and security validation techniques to test cybersecurity resilience and enhance incident detection capabilities.

The role of internal audits extends beyond technical security assessments to include policy enforcement, security awareness training, and compliance verification. Auditors review whether employees follow security policies, password management best practices, and phishing awareness guidelines. Cybersecurity oversight ensures that training programs are regularly updated, security awareness initiatives are measured for effectiveness, and employees are actively engaged in maintaining cybersecurity hygiene.

Third-party risk management is another key area of cybersecurity oversight. Organizations rely on external vendors, cloud service providers, and supply chain partners, which introduces additional security risks. Internal audits evaluate third-party security controls, vendor access policies, and contractual security obligations to ensure that external entities comply with security standards. Vendor risk assessments, third-party penetration testing, and continuous security monitoring help organizations mitigate risks associated with external partnerships.

Cybersecurity metrics and key performance indicators (KPIs) are essential for effective oversight. Security teams track incident detection rates, mean time to detect (MTTD), mean time to respond (MTTR), vulnerability remediation times, compliance scores, and security training completion rates to measure security performance. Audit reports provide executive leadership with data-driven insights into security effectiveness, risk exposure, and areas requiring improvement. Organizations implement dashboard reporting, security scorecards, and compliance heatmaps to visualize security trends and enhance cybersecurity governance.

Cloud security auditing has become a critical focus area due to the widespread adoption of multi-cloud and hybrid cloud environments. Internal audits assess cloud security configurations, identity access controls, encryption policies, and compliance adherence for cloud services. Organizations use cloud security posture management (CSPM) tools, cloud access security brokers (CASBs), and automated compliance scanning to monitor cloud security risks and enforce security best practices. Cybersecurity oversight ensures that cloud governance policies address data sovereignty, access controls, API security, and regulatory compliance in cloud deployments.

Regulatory compliance audits validate whether organizations adhere to industry regulations and legal requirements. HIPAA audits ensure the protection of patient data, PCI DSS audits assess payment card security, GDPR audits verify data privacy protections, and SOX audits evaluate financial reporting security controls. Internal audit teams work closely with compliance officers to ensure that security policies meet legal requirements and prevent regulatory penalties. Audit findings provide recommendations for improving security practices, addressing compliance gaps, and reducing regulatory risks.

Cybersecurity audits must be continuous and adaptive to address the evolving cyber threat landscape. Organizations conduct proactive security assessments, dynamic risk modeling, and predictive analytics to anticipate security challenges and implement preventive controls. Automated threat detection, artificial intelligence-driven security monitoring, and behavioral analytics enhance audit accuracy and security oversight. Governance frameworks require regular security policy reviews, board-level cybersecurity briefings, and executive risk reporting to align cybersecurity with business continuity objectives.

Organizations must foster a culture of accountability and continuous improvement in cybersecurity oversight. Security audits and governance policies should encourage cross-functional collaboration, security innovation, and proactive risk management. Executive leadership must support cybersecurity initiatives by allocating budgets, defining risk tolerance levels, and prioritizing security investments. Organizations that integrate internal audits, security governance, and real-time risk monitoring achieve stronger cybersecurity resilience, reduced threat exposure, and improved regulatory compliance.

Cybersecurity Risk Appetite and Tolerance

Cybersecurity risk appetite and tolerance are fundamental concepts in an organization's risk management strategy. Risk appetite refers to the amount of risk an organization is willing to accept in pursuit of its business objectives, while risk tolerance defines the acceptable deviation from that risk appetite before corrective action is required. Both concepts help organizations balance security measures, business efficiency, and regulatory compliance while making informed decisions about cybersecurity investments, policies, and controls. Establishing a clear risk appetite and tolerance framework enables organizations to prioritize cybersecurity efforts, allocate resources effectively, and maintain resilience against evolving cyber threats.

Defining cybersecurity risk appetite requires executive leadership, security teams, and risk management professionals to collaborate and align security strategies with business objectives. Risk appetite varies by industry, regulatory requirements, and organizational priorities. A financial institution or healthcare provider, for example, may have a low risk appetite due to stringent compliance obligations and the need to protect sensitive customer data. A tech startup or e-commerce platform, on the other hand, may have a higher risk appetite, prioritizing innovation and speed over extensive security controls. Risk appetite must be carefully assessed to ensure that it does not expose the organization to unacceptable risks while allowing business operations to function efficiently.

Risk tolerance defines the threshold at which risk becomes unacceptable, triggering corrective actions or additional security measures. Organizations determine risk tolerance levels based on the likelihood and impact of cybersecurity threats, regulatory penalties, financial consequences, and reputational risks. For example, a company may tolerate a low level of phishing attempts or unsuccessful login attempts, but it may have zero tolerance for unauthorized access to sensitive data or financial fraud incidents. Establishing clear risk tolerance thresholds helps organizations respond effectively to security incidents before they escalate into significant breaches.

A risk assessment framework is essential for determining cybersecurity risk appetite and tolerance. Organizations conduct cyber risk assessments, threat modeling, and business impact analysis (BIA) to evaluate potential threats and their impact on operations. Security teams identify high-risk areas such as critical data assets, privileged access accounts, and external vendor relationships that require stricter security controls. Risk quantification techniques, including risk scoring models, attack surface analysis, and financial impact assessments, help organizations measure risks and define appropriate tolerance levels.

Cybersecurity governance plays a crucial role in managing risk appetite and tolerance. Board members, executives, and security leadership must establish risk policies, define acceptable risk levels, and ensure alignment with business strategy. The Chief Information Security Officer (CISO) is responsible for translating cybersecurity risks into business terms, helping executives make informed decisions about security investments and risk trade-offs. Risk governance frameworks, such as ISO 31000, NIST 800-39, and COBIT, provide structured approaches for defining, assessing, and managing risk appetite and tolerance.

Cyber risk appetite and tolerance must be continuously monitored and adjusted based on evolving threats, technological advancements, and regulatory changes. Organizations use Key Risk Indicators (KRIs) and Key Performance Indicators (KPIs) to track cybersecurity risks, measure security effectiveness, and identify deviations from established risk tolerance levels. Metrics such as incident response times, phishing success rates, system downtime, and compliance violations provide insight into whether risk levels remain within acceptable thresholds. Automated risk dashboards, SIEM analytics, and risk heatmaps enhance real-time risk visibility, enabling organizations to make data-driven security decisions.

Regulatory compliance has a significant impact on risk appetite and tolerance. Many industries must comply with GDPR, HIPAA, PCI DSS, SOX, and NIST 800-53, which impose specific cybersecurity requirements. Organizations with high compliance obligations tend to have lower risk appetite, as regulatory violations result in legal penalties, financial losses, and reputational damage. Compliance-driven risk management ensures that security policies align with data protection laws, breach notification requirements, and audit obligations. Organizations must assess the cost of compliance versus the risk of non-compliance, balancing regulatory adherence with operational efficiency.

Cyber insurance is an important factor influencing risk appetite and tolerance. Organizations assess cyber insurance policies, coverage limits, and claim eligibility criteria to determine how much residual risk they are willing to retain. Cyber insurance helps organizations mitigate financial losses from data breaches, ransomware attacks, and business interruption events. However, insurance alone is not a substitute for strong cybersecurity controls. Security teams must ensure that insurance policies complement existing risk management strategies rather than creating a false sense of security.

Third-party risk management also plays a key role in defining cybersecurity risk appetite. Organizations must assess vendor security practices, supply chain risks, and external dependencies to determine acceptable levels of third-party exposure. Vendor security audits, third-party penetration testing, and continuous monitoring of external partners help organizations enforce security standards and mitigate risks introduced by external entities. Organizations must define risk tolerance for vendor access, data sharing, and cloud service integrations to ensure that third-party relationships align with overall cybersecurity risk posture.

A zero-trust security model is an effective strategy for maintaining cybersecurity risk within acceptable limits. Zero trust operates under the principle of "never trust, always verify," requiring continuous authentication, least privilege access, and network segmentation to minimize attack surfaces. Organizations implementing zero-trust reduce risk exposure, enforce stricter access policies, and prevent lateral movement by attackers. Zero-trust architectures support a low-risk appetite strategy, particularly for organizations handling highly sensitive data, intellectual property, or critical infrastructure systems.

Employee security awareness and training influence cybersecurity risk tolerance by reducing human error, social engineering risks, and insider threats. Organizations conduct regular security training, phishing simulations, and role-based security education to improve risk awareness. A highly trained workforce allows organizations to maintain a slightly higher risk tolerance in areas where human decision-making plays a role in cybersecurity defense. Security governance frameworks ensure that employees, contractors, and executives understand their roles in maintaining cybersecurity hygiene.

Balancing cybersecurity risk appetite and tolerance requires a strategic, risk-based approach that aligns security objectives with business needs. Executive leadership, security teams, compliance officers, and risk managers must work together to define acceptable risk levels, allocate security resources effectively, and ensure continuous risk assessment. Cyber resilience strategies, adaptive security policies, continuous monitoring, and regulatory compliance enforcement, help organizations maintain a well-balanced risk management posture. Organizations that clearly define, monitor, and adjust their cybersecurity risk appetite and tolerance strengthen their overall security governance and ensure long-term business sustainability in an increasingly complex cyber threat landscape.

Cyber Threat Intelligence in Risk Management

Cyber threat intelligence (CTI) plays a crucial role in risk management by providing organizations with actionable insights into cyber threats, attack patterns, and emerging risks. Threat intelligence enables security teams to anticipate, detect, and mitigate cyber threats before they escalate into security incidents. By integrating threat intelligence into risk management frameworks, organizations enhance their ability to protect critical assets, reduce attack surfaces, and make informed security decisions. Effective CTI programs help organizations transition from reactive security measures to a proactive, intelligence-driven approach that strengthens overall cybersecurity resilience.

Cyber threat intelligence is the process of collecting, analyzing, and applying information about threat actors, attack vectors, vulnerabilities, and security trends. Threat intelligence sources include open-source intelligence (OSINT), commercial threat intelligence feeds, government cybersecurity advisories, and industry-specific intelligence-sharing platforms. Organizations leverage machine learning, big data analytics, and behavioral threat modeling to process vast amounts of security data and extract meaningful insights. CTI helps organizations prioritize threats based on risk severity, potential impact, and attack likelihood, enabling efficient resource allocation and risk mitigation strategies.

One of the primary objectives of CTI in risk management is identifying and classifying threats based on intent, capability, and impact. Threat actors range from nation-state attackers, cybercriminal organizations, hacktivists, insider threats, and opportunistic hackers. Each type of threat actor operates with different motivations, such as financial gain, espionage, political activism, or sabotage. Understanding the tactics, techniques, and procedures (TTPs) used by threat actors allows organizations to tailor their security controls and defenses to counter specific threats. Intelligence frameworks such as MITRE ATT&CK provide structured knowledge of attacker behaviors, enabling organizations to map threats to specific countermeasures.

Threat intelligence is categorized into three main types: tactical, operational, and strategic intelligence. Tactical intelligence focuses on specific indicators of compromise (IoCs), such as malicious IP addresses, domain names, hash values, and malware signatures. This type of intelligence is used for real-time threat detection and automated security response. Security tools such as intrusion detection systems (IDS), security information and event management (SIEM) solutions, and endpoint detection and response (EDR) platforms use tactical intelligence to identify and block threats before they can cause damage.

Operational intelligence provides insights into ongoing cyber threats, attack campaigns, and adversary behaviors. Security teams analyze threat actor methodologies, attack timelines, and intrusion kill chains to understand how attackers operate and improve their defensive strategies. Operational intelligence helps organizations strengthen incident response, security monitoring, and digital forensics capabilities by correlating threat data with historical attack patterns. By integrating operational intelligence with cyber kill chain analysis, organizations can disrupt attacks at different stages and minimize their impact.

Strategic intelligence focuses on long-term cybersecurity trends, geopolitical risks, regulatory changes, and industry-specific threat landscapes. This intelligence is used by executive leadership, Chief Information Security Officers (CISOs), and risk management committees to align cybersecurity investments with business priorities. Strategic intelligence informs decision-making related to cybersecurity policies, security budget allocations, and long-term risk mitigation strategies. Organizations use strategic intelligence to assess supply chain risks, third-party vulnerabilities, and emerging technologies that may introduce new security threats.

Threat intelligence plays a critical role in vulnerability management and risk assessment. Organizations use threat intelligence feeds, automated vulnerability scanners, and penetration testing tools to identify exploitable weaknesses in their systems. By correlating vulnerability data with real-world attack intelligence, security teams can prioritize patching efforts, apply compensating security controls, and reduce exposure to high-risk threats. Threat intelligence-driven risk management ensures that security resources are allocated based on the likelihood and impact of a threat being exploited.

Cyber threat intelligence enhances incident response and threat hunting by enabling security teams to detect, analyze, and mitigate threats more effectively. Threat hunting teams leverage threat intelligence reports, IoC lists, and advanced behavioral analytics to proactively search for hidden threats within an organization's network.

Threat-hunting methodologies such as hypothesis-driven investigations, anomaly detection, and adversary emulation help security analysts uncover stealthy cyber threats that evade traditional security controls.

Collaboration and information sharing are essential components of an effective CTI program. Organizations participate in Information Sharing and Analysis Centers (ISACs), threat intelligence exchanges, and government-led cybersecurity initiatives to share and receive threat intelligence. By collaborating with industry peers, regulatory bodies, and law enforcement agencies, organizations gain insights into sector-specific threats, global attack campaigns, and evolving cyber risks. Threat intelligence sharing improves situational awareness, enhances collective defense strategies, and accelerates threat mitigation efforts.

Threat intelligence must be integrated into existing security operations, risk management frameworks, and decision-making processes to maximize its effectiveness. Organizations implement threat intelligence platforms (TIPs), automated threat enrichment, and SIEM integrations to operationalize CTI. By automating threat correlation, incident prioritization, and security alert triage, organizations improve response efficiency and reduce false positives. Threat intelligence-driven security operations centers (SOCs) enhance real-time threat detection, automated incident response, and proactive risk management.

Cyber threat intelligence also supports supply chain security and third-party risk management. Organizations assess the security posture of their vendors, partners, and cloud service providers by analyzing external threat intelligence data, evaluating third-party threat exposure, and conducting continuous security assessments. By monitoring supply chain threats, vendor security incidents, and geopolitical cyber risks, organizations mitigate potential threats originating from external dependencies and third-party integrations.

Artificial intelligence (AI) and machine learning (ML) are transforming the field of cyber threat intelligence by enhancing threat prediction, pattern recognition, and automated threat detection. AI-driven threat intelligence solutions analyze large datasets, detect anomalies, and identify cyberattack trends in real time. Machine learning algorithms improve threat correlation, automated response mechanisms, and adversarial behavior modeling. Organizations leveraging AI-enhanced CTI gain a competitive advantage in predicting, preventing, and responding to cyber threats faster and more accurately.

Effective governance of cyber threat intelligence ensures that intelligence efforts align with business objectives, regulatory requirements, and industry best practices. Security leadership must establish clear threat intelligence policies, define risk tolerance levels, and ensure compliance with data privacy regulations. Organizations must also address ethical considerations, intelligence-sharing agreements, and operational security (OPSEC) measures to prevent intelligence misuse or exposure. Cyber threat intelligence governance ensures that security teams, risk managers, and executive leadership collaborate to enhance cybersecurity resilience.

By incorporating cyber threat intelligence into risk management frameworks, organizations improve their ability to anticipate, detect, and mitigate cyber threats. Threat intelligence-driven security strategies help organizations stay ahead of attackers, prioritize security investments, and adapt to the rapidly evolving threat landscape. Through real-time intelligence, proactive threat hunting, automated security defenses, and collaborative threat sharing, organizations can effectively manage cyber risks and enhance their overall cybersecurity posture.

Cybersecurity Awareness and Training

Cybersecurity awareness and training are essential components of an organization's security strategy. Employees, contractors, and third-party partners must be educated on cybersecurity best practices to reduce human error, prevent security breaches, and enhance overall security resilience. Many cyberattacks exploit human weaknesses through techniques such as phishing, social engineering, and credential theft, making security awareness a fundamental defense mechanism. A well-structured cybersecurity training program ensures that individuals understand their role in protecting sensitive data, identifying security threats, and responding appropriately to cyber incidents.

Cybersecurity awareness programs aim to build a security-conscious culture where employees recognize the importance of cybersecurity in daily operations. Organizations implement training initiatives that educate staff on password management, email security, social engineering attacks, and safe browsing habits. Awareness campaigns reinforce security policies, promote adherence to best practices, and encourage employees to report suspicious activities. Security awareness is not a one-time initiative but a continuous learning process that evolves alongside emerging cyber threats and changing organizational security needs.

Phishing attacks remain one of the most common cyber threats targeting organizations. Employees often receive fraudulent emails designed to trick them into clicking on malicious links, downloading infected attachments, or providing login credentials. Security training programs incorporate simulated phishing exercises to test employee vigilance and improve detection capabilities. Employees who fall for phishing simulations receive additional training to help them recognize suspicious emails and avoid real-world cyber threats. Regular phishing awareness campaigns significantly reduce the likelihood of employees falling victim to email-based attacks.

Strong password management is a fundamental aspect of cybersecurity awareness. Many security breaches occur due to weak, reused, or easily guessable passwords. Employees must be trained on the importance of using strong, unique passwords for each account and adopting password managers to securely store credentials. Organizations enforce multi-factor authentication (MFA) to add an extra layer of security, reducing the risk of account compromise. Security training programs emphasize the dangers of credential reuse and educate users on how to create and manage secure passwords effectively.

Social engineering attacks manipulate human psychology to bypass security controls. Attackers use pretexting, baiting, tailgating, and impersonation techniques to deceive employees into divulging sensitive information or granting unauthorized access. Security awareness training educates employees on how to recognize and respond to social engineering attempts. Employees learn to verify caller identities, scrutinize unexpected requests for sensitive information, and follow strict verification protocols before sharing data or granting access. A security-conscious workforce acts as the first line of defense against social engineering threats.

Data protection and handling procedures are critical topics in cybersecurity training. Employees must understand data classification policies, encryption requirements, and secure data transfer protocols to prevent unauthorized access and data leaks. Training programs emphasize the importance of secure file sharing, restricted access permissions, and compliance with data protection regulations such as GDPR, HIPAA, and PCI DSS. Security teams conduct role-based training to educate employees on handling sensitive information according to regulatory and organizational requirements.

Insider threats pose significant security risks, whether intentional or accidental. Employees with access to critical systems and data can inadvertently expose sensitive information through misconfigurations, accidental data sharing, or poor security practices. Cybersecurity training addresses insider threat awareness, access control best practices, and reporting mechanisms for suspicious activities. Organizations establish least privilege access models and user activity monitoring to minimize insider threat risks. Training programs help employees understand the consequences of mishandling sensitive data and the importance of adhering to security policies.

Secure use of corporate devices and personal devices in the workplace is a key focus of cybersecurity awareness. Organizations implement bring your own device (BYOD) policies, mobile device management (MDM) solutions, and endpoint security measures to protect corporate data on personal devices. Employees must be trained on secure remote access practices, virtual private networks (VPNs), and endpoint protection software to prevent unauthorized access and malware infections. Training sessions cover safe Wi-Fi usage, device encryption, and best practices for securing mobile applications and cloud storage accounts.

Incident response training ensures that employees know how to react in the event of a security breach or cyberattack. Organizations establish incident reporting procedures, escalation protocols, and crisis management workflows to streamline security response efforts. Employees receive guidance on how to report phishing emails, suspicious network activity, lost or stolen devices, and unauthorized access attempts. Security teams conduct tabletop exercises, red team drills, and cyber crisis simulations to improve incident response coordination and test employee preparedness.

Cloud security awareness is increasingly important as organizations transition to cloud-based services and applications. Employees must understand cloud security risks, shared responsibility models, and secure cloud access policies. Training programs cover secure file storage, cloud access controls, and data sharing best practices to prevent unauthorized data exposure. Organizations enforce identity and access management (IAM) policies, audit logging, and cloud security posture management (CSPM) solutions to enhance cloud security awareness and governance.

Third-party security awareness ensures that vendors, contractors, and external partners adhere to the organization's cybersecurity policies and security requirements. Organizations conduct vendor security training, third-party risk assessments, and security awareness briefings to ensure compliance with security controls. Security agreements and contractual obligations require external parties to follow secure access policies, encryption standards, and data protection measures. Regular security audits and compliance assessments verify that third-party entities maintain strong cybersecurity practices.

Cybersecurity training effectiveness is measured using security awareness assessments, phishing campaign results, policy compliance rates, and security quiz scores. Organizations collect feedback from employees to improve training content and tailor security education to different roles and departments. Security teams track employee-reported security incidents, password policy adherence, and response times to simulated cyber threats to evaluate training success. Continuous improvement ensures that cybersecurity training programs remain relevant, engaging, and aligned with evolving security risks.

Security awareness culture is reinforced through executive leadership support, ongoing security communications, and employee engagement initiatives. Organizations establish cybersecurity awareness months, internal security newsletters, security champions programs, and gamified training modules to encourage active participation in cybersecurity education. Leadership involvement in security awareness programs demonstrates organizational commitment to cybersecurity best practices and risk reduction.

Cybersecurity awareness and training must be an ongoing effort, integrated into daily business operations and reinforced through regular security initiatives. A well-trained workforce significantly reduces cybersecurity risks, prevents security incidents, and enhances organizational resilience against evolving threats. Organizations that prioritize cybersecurity education create a security-conscious culture where employees, executives, and stakeholders actively contribute to a strong and proactive security posture.

Security Operations Center (SOC) Governance

Security Operations Center (SOC) governance is essential for ensuring that cybersecurity operations align with an organization's risk management framework, business objectives, and regulatory compliance requirements. The SOC serves as the central hub for monitoring, detecting, analyzing, and responding to cybersecurity threats in real time. Effective governance ensures that SOC processes, technologies, and personnel operate efficiently to protect critical assets, prevent security breaches, and enhance organizational resilience against cyber threats.

A well-structured SOC governance model defines roles, responsibilities, policies, and procedures that guide the operation of the security center. Governance ensures that the SOC follows industry best practices, integrates with the organization's broader security strategy, and continuously improves its capabilities. The governance framework establishes accountability for security operations, ensuring that security analysts, incident responders, and threat intelligence teams work together in a coordinated manner. It also defines escalation paths, reporting structures, and decision-making processes for handling security incidents.

SOC governance includes developing and enforcing security monitoring policies that outline how security events are detected, analyzed, and responded to. Organizations establish rules of engagement, incident classification criteria, and response protocols to standardize threat detection and response activities. Governance frameworks align SOC policies with NIST Cybersecurity Framework, ISO 27001, CIS Controls, and MITRE ATT&CK to ensure that security operations follow globally recognized best practices.

The effectiveness of a SOC depends on well-defined metrics and key performance indicators (KPIs) that measure its performance. Governance frameworks establish mean time to detect (MTTD), mean time to respond (MTTR), false positive rates, threat detection accuracy, and compliance adherence as key SOC performance metrics. Regular performance assessments ensure that SOC operations remain efficient, proactive, and aligned with evolving cyber threats. Organizations implement automated dashboards, SOC maturity models, and continuous monitoring tools to track operational effectiveness and optimize security response workflows.

Security event monitoring is a core function of the SOC, and governance ensures that monitoring activities cover all critical assets, including networks, endpoints, cloud environments, applications, and third-party integrations. Organizations deploy Security Information and Event Management (SIEM) solutions, threat intelligence platforms, and behavioral analytics tools to aggregate and analyze security event data. Governance ensures that security alerts are prioritized based on severity, business impact, and potential risks, reducing alert fatigue and allowing analysts to focus on high-priority threats.

Incident response governance establishes structured workflows for handling security incidents from detection to resolution. Organizations develop incident response playbooks, escalation procedures, and communication protocols to ensure consistency in incident handling. Governance frameworks define roles and responsibilities for incident responders, forensic investigators, legal teams, and executive leadership to coordinate response efforts effectively. Regular tabletop exercises, red team/blue team drills, and cyber crisis simulations help SOC teams refine their response capabilities and improve incident readiness.

Threat intelligence integration is a key aspect of SOC governance. Organizations leverage internal threat intelligence, open-source intelligence (OSINT), commercial threat feeds, and government cybersecurity advisories to enhance threat detection capabilities. Governance frameworks define threat intelligence sharing policies, data classification standards, and intelligence fusion techniques to ensure that threat intelligence is actionable and relevant. By integrating threat intelligence with SIEM platforms, intrusion detection systems (IDS), and endpoint detection and response (EDR) solutions, SOC teams gain real-time visibility into evolving cyber threats.

SOC governance extends to cloud security monitoring, as organizations increasingly adopt cloud-based services and hybrid IT environments. Governance frameworks establish cloud security policies, access controls, and continuous compliance monitoring to protect cloud workloads from cyber threats. Organizations implement cloud security posture management (CSPM) solutions, cloud-native security analytics, and API security monitoring to detect misconfigurations, unauthorized access, and data exposure risks. SOC teams enforce zero-trust security models and cloud segmentation strategies to enhance cloud security governance.

Identity and access management (IAM) governance is another critical component of SOC operations. Organizations enforce privileged access monitoring, multi-factor authentication (MFA) policies, and identity behavior analytics to prevent unauthorized access to critical systems. Governance ensures that role-based access control (RBAC), just-in-time (JIT) privilege escalation, and session monitoring are implemented to protect sensitive security operations. SOC teams continuously monitor user access logs, authentication anomalies, and insider threat indicators to detect potential security violations.

SOC governance also addresses third-party risk management, ensuring that vendors, contractors, and external partners comply with security policies. Organizations conduct third-party security assessments, continuous monitoring of external access, and security audits to enforce cybersecurity standards across the supply chain. Governance frameworks require vendor security agreements, compliance attestations, and security posture assessments to mitigate risks associated with third-party integrations.

Automation and orchestration play a significant role in SOC efficiency, and governance ensures that security automation aligns with operational objectives. Organizations implement Security Orchestration, Automation, and Response (SOAR) solutions to automate threat response workflows, reduce manual intervention, and enhance incident resolution speed. Governance frameworks establish rules for automated threat containment, real-time remediation actions, and predefined security workflows to optimize SOC efficiency. Automated security controls help SOC teams handle large-scale cyber threats while maintaining operational agility.

Compliance and regulatory adherence are central to SOC governance. Organizations align security monitoring and incident response practices with GDPR, HIPAA, PCI DSS, SOX, and other regulatory requirements. Governance frameworks define security audit requirements, log retention policies, and breach notification procedures to ensure compliance with legal and industry standards. Regular compliance audits, security assessments, and governance reviews help organizations maintain continuous security validation and regulatory readiness.

SOC governance includes security training and workforce development to enhance the capabilities of security analysts, incident responders, and threat hunters. Organizations implement continuous learning programs, cybersecurity certifications, hands-on training exercises, and attack simulation labs to upskill SOC personnel. Governance frameworks require that SOC staff participate in ongoing cybersecurity education, advanced threat detection training, and real-world attack scenario testing to maintain expertise in handling evolving cyber threats.

Cybersecurity leadership and executive oversight ensure that SOC governance aligns with business objectives, risk management strategies, and organizational priorities. Chief Information Security Officers (CISOs), security committees, and executive leadership teams provide guidance on security investments, SOC resource allocation, and long-term cybersecurity roadmaps. Governance frameworks establish risk reporting mechanisms, executive-level security briefings, and key security metrics presentations to keep leadership informed about cybersecurity posture and SOC performance.

Continuous improvement is a fundamental principle of SOC governance. Organizations implement post-incident reviews, security gap assessments, and cybersecurity maturity evaluations to identify areas for improvement. Security teams analyze incident response effectiveness, threat detection accuracy, and security policy adherence to enhance SOC capabilities. Governance frameworks require regular SOC audits, process optimizations, and strategic security planning to adapt to emerging threats and maintain long-term cybersecurity resilience.

By implementing structured SOC governance frameworks, organizations ensure operational efficiency, regulatory compliance, and proactive threat management. Governance enables SOC teams to leverage advanced security technologies, automate security operations, integrate threat intelligence, and align cybersecurity efforts with business risk strategies. Strong governance transforms the SOC into a highly effective security operations unit capable of detecting, analyzing, and mitigating cyber threats with precision and speed.

Regulatory Trends and Future Compliance Challenges

Regulatory trends in cybersecurity and data privacy are evolving rapidly, driven by increasing cyber threats, technological advancements, and growing concerns over data protection. Governments and regulatory bodies worldwide are implementing stricter laws to ensure that organizations take responsibility for securing sensitive information, maintaining transparency, and mitigating cybersecurity risks. Compliance requirements are no longer limited to specific industries but now apply to a broad range of businesses, from financial institutions and healthcare providers to technology companies and critical infrastructure operators. Organizations must stay ahead of regulatory developments to avoid penalties, strengthen their security posture, and maintain customer trust.

One of the most significant regulatory trends is the increasing globalization of data privacy laws. The General Data Protection Regulation (GDPR) set a new standard for data privacy when it came into effect in 2018, influencing other jurisdictions to adopt similar regulations. Countries such as Brazil (LGPD), Canada (CPPA), India (DPDP Act), and China (PIPL) have introduced data protection laws that mirror GDPR principles, requiring organizations to implement strict data security measures, obtain explicit consent for data collection, and ensure data subject rights. The challenge for multinational organizations is complying with multiple, sometimes conflicting, data protection laws while maintaining business operations across different regions.

The patchwork of U.S. state-level privacy laws is another emerging trend in compliance. Unlike GDPR, which establishes a unified privacy framework for the European Union, the United States lacks a federal data privacy law. Instead, states such as California (CCPA/CPRA), Virginia (VCDPA), Colorado (CPA), and Utah (UCPA) have enacted their own privacy regulations, creating compliance challenges for businesses operating in multiple states. Each state law has unique requirements for data access, opt-out mechanisms, and consumer rights, making compliance a complex and resource-intensive process. Future regulations may include a federal U.S. privacy law that harmonizes data protection requirements nationwide, but until then, organizations must navigate a fragmented regulatory landscape.

Emerging regulations are placing greater emphasis on cybersecurity governance and incident reporting. The U.S. Securities and Exchange Commission (SEC) has introduced new cybersecurity disclosure rules that require publicly traded companies to report material cybersecurity incidents within four business days. This regulation aims to improve transparency for investors and ensure that cybersecurity risks are managed at the executive level. Similarly, the Cyber Incident Reporting for Critical Infrastructure Act (CIRCIA) mandates that critical infrastructure organizations report significant cyber incidents to the Cybersecurity and Infrastructure Security Agency (CISA) within 72 hours. These regulations signal a shift toward mandatory incident disclosure rather than voluntary reporting, increasing pressure on organizations to enhance their incident detection, response, and reporting mechanisms.

Artificial intelligence (AI) and automated decision-making systems are raising new compliance challenges. As organizations integrate AI into cybersecurity, finance, healthcare, and other sectors, regulators are introducing AI governance frameworks to ensure transparency, fairness, and accountability. The EU AI Act is set to become one of the world's first comprehensive AI regulations, classifying AI systems based on risk levels and imposing strict compliance requirements for high-risk AI applications. Organizations deploying AI-powered security tools must ensure that these technologies comply with bias detection, explainability, and ethical AI principles, avoiding regulatory penalties and reputational damage.

Supply chain security and third-party risk management are becoming central to regulatory frameworks. High-profile attacks, such as the SolarWinds supply chain breach, have demonstrated how vulnerabilities in third-party vendors can compromise entire networks. Governments and regulators are responding by requiring organizations to conduct third-party security assessments, enforce contractual cybersecurity obligations, and monitor vendor security postures continuously. The NIST Cybersecurity Framework (CSF 2.0) and ISO 27036 provide guidelines for securing supply chains, while regulations such as DORA (Digital Operational Resilience Act) in the EU impose strict cybersecurity requirements on financial sector vendors and service providers.

Cloud security compliance is becoming more complex as organizations migrate to cloud-based environments. Regulations are now expanding their scope to cover cloud service providers (CSPs), shared responsibility models, and multi-cloud security risks. The European Union's proposed Cybersecurity Certification Scheme for Cloud Services (EUCS) aims to standardize cloud security certifications, ensuring that cloud providers meet strict cybersecurity requirements. In the United States, the Federal Risk and Authorization Management Program (FedRAMP) continues to set compliance benchmarks for cloud services used by federal agencies. Organizations must ensure data encryption, access control, and regulatory compliance in cloud environments, balancing security and operational flexibility.

The rise of ransomware attacks and financial cybercrime is prompting governments to introduce stricter regulations on cybersecurity resilience and incident response. The U.S. Treasury Department's Office of Foreign Assets Control (OFAC) has issued guidance warning organizations against making ransomware payments to sanctioned entities, increasing the legal and financial risks of ransomware incidents. The Financial Action Task Force (FATF) and Bank for International Settlements (BIS) are pushing for stronger cybersecurity regulations in the financial sector, requiring banks and financial institutions to enhance fraud detection, secure payment systems, and implement anti-money laundering (AML) measures for cryptocurrency transactions.

Critical infrastructure security is a growing priority for regulators, as cyber threats increasingly target energy grids, transportation systems, water treatment facilities, and healthcare providers. The U.S. National Cybersecurity Strategy (2023) introduces new directives for securing critical infrastructure, including mandatory cybersecurity risk assessments, zero-trust architecture adoption, and government-industry collaboration on threat intelligence sharing. The EU Network and Information Security Directive 2 (NIS2) imposes stricter cybersecurity requirements on essential services providers, extending compliance obligations to telecommunications, digital service providers, and cloud computing sectors. Organizations operating in critical infrastructure sectors must continuously assess cybersecurity risks, implement robust incident response plans, and comply with sector-specific security regulations.

Regulatory enforcement is becoming more aggressive, with higher fines, stricter penalties, and increased regulatory scrutiny. GDPR regulators have issued record-breaking fines against companies such as Amazon, Meta, and Google for non-compliance, setting a precedent for stricter data protection enforcement. The U.S. Federal Trade Commission (FTC) has also expanded its enforcement actions, holding organizations accountable for inadequate cybersecurity measures and misleading data privacy practices. Organizations must adopt a proactive compliance strategy, ensuring continuous security audits, data protection impact assessments, and regulatory alignment to avoid enforcement actions.

Future compliance challenges will require organizations to embrace automation, artificial intelligence, and continuous compliance monitoring to keep pace with evolving regulatory demands. RegTech (Regulatory Technology) solutions are emerging to help organizations manage compliance requirements efficiently, leveraging AI-driven compliance analytics, automated reporting tools, and real-time risk assessments. Organizations must build adaptive compliance programs, integrate security frameworks, and ensure executive-level cybersecurity governance to navigate the increasingly complex regulatory landscape.

As cybersecurity threats become more sophisticated, regulatory frameworks will continue to evolve, demanding higher security standards, increased transparency, and proactive risk management. Organizations that stay ahead of regulatory trends, invest in security compliance, and implement strong governance frameworks will be better positioned to manage future compliance challenges and maintain trust with regulators, customers, and stakeholders.

Artificial Intelligence in Cybersecurity Risk Management

Artificial intelligence (AI) is transforming cybersecurity risk management by enhancing threat detection, automating security operations, and improving response capabilities. Traditional cybersecurity approaches often struggle to keep up with the scale and complexity of modern cyber threats. AI-driven security solutions leverage machine learning, predictive analytics, and automation to identify risks in real-time, adapt to emerging threats, and optimize security processes. Organizations are increasingly integrating AI into their cybersecurity strategies to enhance risk assessment, reduce response times, and improve overall cyber resilience.

One of the most significant applications of AI in cybersecurity risk management is threat detection and anomaly identification. AI-powered security information and event management (SIEM) systems, endpoint detection and response (EDR) platforms, and intrusion detection systems (IDS) analyze vast amounts of security data to identify patterns, deviations, and potential security incidents. Machine learning algorithms continuously learn from historical attack data, enabling them to detect previously unknown threats, including zero-day vulnerabilities and advanced persistent threats (APTs). AI-driven behavioral analytics monitor user activity, network traffic, and system logs to detect suspicious behavior, privilege escalation attempts, and data exfiltration in real time.

AI enhances predictive threat intelligence by analyzing global threat trends, attack campaigns, and emerging vulnerabilities. Traditional cybersecurity defenses rely on signature-based detection, which is ineffective against novel threats. AI models use heuristic analysis, natural language processing (NLP), and deep learning to assess threat intelligence feeds, dark web activity, and hacker forums for indicators of compromise (IoCs). AI-driven threat intelligence enables security teams to anticipate cyberattacks, assess threat actor motivations, and prioritize risk mitigation strategies before an attack occurs.

Automation powered by AI significantly improves incident response and remediation. Security operations centers (SOCs) face an overwhelming number of security alerts, many of which are false positives. AI-driven Security Orchestration, Automation, and Response (SOAR) platforms streamline threat investigation by correlating security events, classifying alerts, and automating response workflows. AI-driven automation can quarantine infected endpoints, block malicious IP addresses, and enforce access restrictions without requiring manual intervention. This reduces the burden on security analysts, allowing them to focus on high-priority threats and strategic risk management.

AI also enhances risk assessment and vulnerability management by identifying security gaps in IT infrastructure, applications, and cloud environments. Traditional vulnerability assessments rely on periodic scans and manual analysis, which can miss critical risks. AI-driven vulnerability assessment tools analyze code repositories, system configurations, and third-party integrations to detect potential security weaknesses before they are exploited. AI models predict which vulnerabilities are most likely to be exploited based on historical attack data, enabling security teams to prioritize patching efforts, allocate resources effectively, and reduce risk exposure.

Identity and access management (IAM) benefits from AI-powered adaptive authentication and behavioral analysis. AI-driven IAM solutions analyze user login patterns, device behavior, and contextual risk factors to enforce risk-based authentication and continuous access validation. If an AI system detects anomalous behavior, such as an employee logging in from an unfamiliar location or a sudden spike in data access requests, it can trigger additional security measures such as multi-factor authentication (MFA), session termination, or account lockdown. AI-powered IAM reduces the risk of unauthorized access while enhancing user experience by minimizing unnecessary security prompts.

AI plays a crucial role in fraud detection and financial cybersecurity. Financial institutions, e-commerce platforms, and payment processors use AI-powered models to detect credit card fraud, insider trading, and money laundering schemes. Machine learning algorithms analyze transaction data, spending behaviors, and historical fraud patterns to flag anomalous financial activity and potential fraud attempts. AI-driven fraud detection systems continuously adapt to new attack techniques and fraud methodologies, reducing financial losses and regulatory risks.

Cloud security is another area where AI improves cybersecurity risk management. Cloud environments introduce unique security challenges, including misconfigurations, unauthorized access, and insecure APIs. AI-driven Cloud Security Posture Management (CSPM) solutions monitor cloud environments in real time, detecting security misconfigurations, enforcing compliance policies, and recommending corrective actions. AI-powered automated cloud security audits and compliance assessments help organizations maintain a secure cloud infrastructure while adhering to industry standards such as ISO 27001, NIST 800-53, and SOC 2.

AI-driven insider threat detection helps organizations prevent malicious or accidental data leaks, intellectual property theft, and unauthorized system access. Traditional security measures often fail to detect sophisticated insider threats, as they rely on predefined rules rather than dynamic behavior analysis. AI models analyze employee behavior, email communications, and system interactions to detect anomalies that indicate potential insider threats. Organizations use AI-powered data loss prevention (DLP) tools, automated risk scoring, and anomaly detection systems to identify high-risk employees, unauthorized data transfers, and policy violations.

Cybersecurity compliance and regulatory adherence are also improved through AI-driven automation. Organizations must comply with stringent data protection laws such as GDPR, HIPAA, PCI DSS, and CCPA, which require continuous monitoring, audit logging, and security policy enforcement. AI-powered compliance tools analyze security controls, automate compliance reporting, and detect policy violations in real time. Automated compliance assessments reduce manual effort, improve regulatory adherence, and enhance risk visibility across IT environments.

One of the biggest challenges in AI-driven cybersecurity is adversarial AI and evasion techniques. Cybercriminals are developing AI-powered attack methods, including AI-generated phishing emails, deepfake impersonation, and automated vulnerability exploitation. Attackers use machine learning to evade detection, manipulate AI models, and bypass traditional security defenses. Organizations must develop robust AI governance frameworks, adversarial AI defenses, and continuous security validation techniques to mitigate the risks associated with malicious AI-driven attacks.

Ethical considerations and AI bias in cybersecurity present another challenge. AI models rely on large datasets for training, which may contain biases that affect security decisions. Biased AI models can result in false positives, inaccurate threat classification, and discriminatory security policies. Organizations must implement explainable AI (XAI), bias detection mechanisms, and ethical AI governance to ensure that AI-driven security decisions are fair, transparent, and accountable.

AI is rapidly transforming cybersecurity risk management, offering advanced threat detection, automated incident response, and real-time risk assessment. Organizations that integrate AI into their cybersecurity strategies benefit from faster threat identification, improved security operations efficiency, and proactive risk mitigation. However, as AI adoption increases, security teams must address challenges related to adversarial AI threats, AI bias, and regulatory compliance. By leveraging AI-powered security tools, continuous learning algorithms, and ethical AI governance, organizations can enhance their cybersecurity posture and stay ahead of emerging cyber risks.

Blockchain and GRC Applications

Blockchain technology is transforming Governance, Risk, and Compliance (GRC) by introducing transparency, security, and automation into regulatory and risk management processes. Traditionally, GRC frameworks rely on centralized databases, manual auditing, and trust-based verification mechanisms. Blockchain's decentralized and immutable nature enhances the integrity of records, automates compliance reporting, and reduces fraud risks. Organizations are exploring blockchain applications to improve regulatory adherence, data integrity, identity management, and risk assessment.

One of the primary benefits of blockchain in GRC is immutability and auditability. Regulatory frameworks require organizations to maintain tamper-proof records of transactions, access logs, and compliance reports. Blockchain stores records in chronologically linked blocks, preventing unauthorized modifications or data manipulation. Regulators and auditors can access blockchain-based real-time compliance records, smart contract execution logs, and automated audit trails, reducing the need for manual verification. This enhances transparency, regulatory accountability, and risk oversight.

Smart contracts play a crucial role in automating compliance enforcement and regulatory reporting. These self-executing contracts operate on predefined rules coded into the blockchain, ensuring that transactions comply with legal and regulatory standards. Organizations use smart contracts for automated risk assessments, compliance checks, and fraud detection. For example, in financial services, smart contracts ensure that transactions meet anti-money laundering (AML) and know-your-customer (KYC) requirements before processing payments. Automating these processes reduces the risk of human error, enhances efficiency, and ensures real-time compliance.

Identity and access management (IAM) benefit from blockchain's decentralized identity solutions. Traditional IAM systems rely on centralized databases vulnerable to cyberattacks, credential theft, and unauthorized access. Blockchain-based self-sovereign identity (SSI) models allow users to control their digital identities, authentication credentials, and access permissions without relying on a central authority. Organizations implement blockchain-based multi-factor authentication (MFA), biometric verification, and decentralized identity verification to enhance security and privacy while maintaining compliance with GDPR, HIPAA, and ISO 27001.

Blockchain enhances supply chain security and third-party risk management by ensuring transparency and traceability. Organizations must verify that vendors, suppliers, and subcontractors comply with security standards and ethical sourcing requirements. Blockchain records every transaction in the supply chain, preventing fraud, unauthorized modifications, and compliance violations. Regulatory bodies and industry consortia use blockchain to track product authenticity, enforce supply chain security standards, and verify regulatory adherence in real time. Industries such as pharmaceuticals, automotive, and food safety leverage blockchain for counterfeit prevention, traceability, and compliance reporting.

Fraud prevention and financial integrity benefit from blockchain's decentralized and cryptographic security mechanisms. Traditional financial transactions are susceptible to manipulation, double spending, and insider fraud. Blockchain ensures that every transaction is cryptographically signed, timestamped, and permanently recorded, reducing the risk of fraud and financial misconduct. Regulatory authorities use blockchain to enforce real-time transaction monitoring, AML compliance, and fraud risk assessment. Organizations integrate blockchain with regulatory compliance solutions, risk management platforms, and forensic investigation tools to improve financial oversight.

Blockchain-based regulatory sandboxes are emerging as a tool for testing and validating compliance solutions in a controlled environment. Regulators and financial institutions use blockchain-powered sandboxes to simulate regulatory scenarios, assess compliance automation, and evaluate risk models before implementing them in real-world applications. These sandboxes allow organizations to test smart contract governance, automated compliance workflows, and regulatory reporting frameworks while ensuring alignment with GDPR, PCI DSS, and Basel III financial regulations.

Data protection and privacy regulations require organizations to manage data access, retention, and consent management securely. Blockchain supports privacy-enhancing technologies (PETs) such as zero-knowledge proofs (ZKPs) and homomorphic encryption to ensure compliance with data protection laws while maintaining security. Organizations implement blockchain-based consent management platforms, tokenized access control, and decentralized data governance models to comply with privacy regulations such as CCPA, LGPD, and PIPL. Blockchain enables individuals to control their personal data, revoke access rights, and audit how their information is used.

Cyber risk management benefits from blockchain's ability to enhance threat intelligence sharing, incident response coordination, and cyber risk analytics. Organizations use blockchain to securely share cyber threat intelligence, track vulnerabilities, and enforce collaborative security frameworks. Blockchain-based cyber risk registries store real-time threat intelligence, breach indicators, and attack signatures, allowing organizations to detect, analyze, and mitigate cyber risks efficiently. Security operations centers (SOCs) leverage blockchain for tamper-proof log management, forensic evidence integrity, and automated incident response coordination.

Regulatory reporting and audit automation are streamlined using blockchain-powered compliance platforms. Traditional audit processes involve manual data reconciliation, document verification, and third-party attestations, which are time-consuming and prone to errors. Blockchain automates compliance reporting by digitally signing regulatory filings, verifying financial disclosures, and generating immutable audit logs. Regulatory bodies, financial institutions, and corporate governance teams use blockchain-based compliance platforms to accelerate reporting, reduce audit costs, and improve regulatory transparency.

Blockchain applications in smart governance and risk frameworks enable organizations to build dynamic, self-executing regulatory policies. Smart contracts enforce real-time policy compliance, automate risk scoring, and trigger security controls based on predefined risk thresholds. Organizations integrate blockchain with GRC platforms, risk analytics engines, and compliance dashboards to ensure continuous security monitoring, regulatory adaptation, and governance automation.

Emerging blockchain regulations and standardization efforts will shape the future of blockchain-enabled GRC solutions. Regulatory agencies are defining legal frameworks for blockchain governance, digital asset regulations, and decentralized finance (DeFi) compliance. Governments and industry consortia are developing blockchain security standards, cryptographic frameworks, and regulatory guidance to ensure that blockchain applications comply with international cybersecurity and risk management requirements.

Blockchain and GRC applications continue to evolve, enabling organizations to enhance security, compliance automation, fraud prevention, and risk transparency. By leveraging immutable audit trails, smart contract governance, decentralized identity, and automated regulatory reporting, organizations can build a resilient, risk-aware, and compliance-driven cybersecurity framework.

Cybersecurity Ethics and Legal Considerations

Cybersecurity ethics and legal considerations play a critical role in shaping how organizations and individuals navigate digital security challenges. As cyber threats evolve, ethical principles and legal frameworks guide decision-making in areas such as data privacy, surveillance, cybercrime prevention, and digital rights. Organizations must balance security, privacy, compliance, and ethical responsibility to ensure fair, lawful, and transparent cybersecurity practices. Ethical considerations influence policies on data collection, user consent, algorithmic fairness, and responsible disclosure, while legal frameworks establish the boundaries of lawful cybersecurity operations, regulatory compliance, and accountability.

One of the most pressing ethical issues in cybersecurity is privacy and data protection. Organizations collect and store vast amounts of user data, including personal, financial, and behavioral information. Ethical cybersecurity practices require organizations to respect user privacy, obtain informed consent, and limit data collection to necessary purposes. Legal regulations such as GDPR (General Data Protection Regulation), CCPA (California Consumer Privacy Act), and HIPAA (Health Insurance Portability and Accountability Act) enforce privacy rights and set strict guidelines for data storage, processing, and sharing. Ethical dilemmas arise when organizations collect excessive user data, track online behavior without consent, or fail to secure personal information against breaches.

The ethical implications of surveillance and monitoring in cybersecurity are another key consideration. Governments and corporations deploy network monitoring, AI-driven threat detection, and digital forensics tools to prevent cyber threats. While surveillance helps detect malicious activity, insider threats, and cyberattacks, it also raises concerns about individual privacy, mass data collection, and potential abuse of power. Ethical cybersecurity frameworks require organizations to implement proportional, transparent, and legally justified monitoring policies while respecting civil liberties, digital rights, and employee privacy. Legal frameworks such as the U.S. Electronic Communications Privacy Act (ECPA) and the EU's ePrivacy Directive regulate surveillance practices to prevent misuse and unauthorized data collection.

Cybersecurity professionals must adhere to ethical hacking principles when conducting security assessments. Ethical hacking involves penetration testing, vulnerability assessments, and red team exercises to identify security weaknesses before attackers exploit them. However, ethical concerns arise when organizations fail to obtain proper authorization, exceed the scope of testing, or exploit vulnerabilities for personal gain. Professional ethical codes such as the Certified Ethical Hacker (CEH) Code of Conduct and the ISC2 Code of Ethics emphasize honesty, integrity, and responsible disclosure.

Responsible vulnerability disclosure ensures that security researchers report security flaws to organizations or regulatory bodies instead of selling them on dark web marketplaces or using them maliciously.

The legal landscape of cybercrime and digital forensics establishes boundaries for ethical cybersecurity practices. Cybercrime laws such as the Computer Fraud and Abuse Act (CFAA), EU Cybercrime Directive, and Budapest Convention on Cybercrime define legal consequences for activities such as hacking, identity theft, data breaches, and cyber espionage. Cybersecurity professionals must follow legal guidelines when investigating cyber incidents, collecting digital evidence, and attributing cyberattacks. Digital forensics requires strict adherence to chain of custody procedures, evidence integrity protocols, and privacy laws to ensure that cybersecurity investigations remain legally admissible in court.

Artificial intelligence (AI) in cybersecurity presents ethical challenges related to bias, transparency, and accountability. AI-driven security tools analyze network behavior, detect threats, and automate risk assessments, but biases in AI models can result in false positives, discriminatory security policies, and unfair profiling. Ethical AI principles require organizations to ensure fairness, avoid algorithmic discrimination, and provide transparency in automated decision-making. Legal considerations include AI governance regulations, data protection laws, and human oversight requirements to prevent misuse of AI-driven surveillance, automated threat attribution, and privacy violations.

The ethical dilemma of cybersecurity and national security involves balancing public safety, government surveillance, and digital freedoms. Governments enforce cybersecurity laws to protect critical infrastructure, prevent cyberterrorism, and combat state-sponsored cyberattacks. However, policies such as state-sponsored hacking, encryption backdoors, and internet censorship raise ethical concerns about government overreach, digital sovereignty, and human rights violations. Laws such as the USA PATRIOT Act, China's Cybersecurity Law, and the EU's Network and Information Security Directive (NIS2) regulate cyber intelligence, law enforcement access to data, and cross-border cybercrime cooperation. Ethical cybersecurity frameworks promote transparent governance, accountable cyber policies, and respect for global digital rights.

Cybersecurity ethics extend to corporate responsibility and whistleblower protection. Organizations face ethical dilemmas when responding to security breaches, insider threats, and corporate data misuse. Ethical corporate policies require organizations to disclose data breaches, protect whistleblowers, and prioritize cybersecurity investments. High-profile cases such as Edward Snowden's NSA revelations and Facebook's Cambridge Analytica scandal highlight the tension between corporate secrecy, government surveillance, and public interest. Laws such as the Whistleblower Protection Act and GDPR's breach notification requirements enforce accountability and transparency in cybersecurity governance.

The ethics of ransomware payments present complex challenges for organizations facing cyber extortion. Ransomware attackers demand payments in exchange for decrypting stolen data, often targeting hospitals, financial institutions, and government agencies. Paying ransoms may incentivize further attacks and fund criminal organizations, terrorist networks, or sanctioned entities. Governments such as the U.S. Treasury Department's Office of Foreign Assets Control (OFAC) have issued warnings against paying ransoms to cybercriminal groups linked to sanctioned states. Ethical cybersecurity policies discourage ransomware payments, promote data recovery strategies, and enforce cyber resilience instead of funding illegal activities.

Legal and ethical concerns in cloud security and third-party risk management arise as organizations rely on cloud providers, software-as-a-service (SaaS) platforms, and external vendors to handle sensitive data. Organizations must ensure that third-party security practices comply with regulatory frameworks such as ISO 27001, SOC 2, and FedRAMP. Ethical considerations include ensuring vendor transparency, protecting shared data, and holding third parties accountable for security breaches. Contracts and data protection agreements (DPAs) define legal responsibilities for cloud providers, minimizing liability risks and ensuring compliance with international cybersecurity laws.

Cybersecurity education and ethical responsibility shape the future of digital security. Universities, certification bodies, and professional organizations incorporate cybersecurity ethics courses, responsible disclosure training, and legal compliance awareness into security programs. Ethical leadership in cybersecurity encourages professionals to act with integrity, report security violations, and advocate for responsible security policies. Organizations enforce ethical security policies, compliance frameworks, and diversity in cybersecurity teams to promote fair and transparent cybersecurity practices.

Cybersecurity ethics and legal considerations continue to evolve as new technologies, regulations, and global threats emerge. Organizations must align security policies with ethical principles, comply with legal frameworks, and balance cybersecurity objectives with individual rights. Ethical cybersecurity governance ensures that security professionals, corporations, and governments operate responsibly, protecting digital ecosystems while upholding legal and ethical standards.

Data Classification and Protection Policies

Data classification and protection policies are fundamental to a robust cybersecurity strategy, ensuring that sensitive information is identified, categorized, and safeguarded against unauthorized access, loss, or theft. Organizations handle vast amounts of data, including personally identifiable information (PII), financial records, intellectual property, and confidential business information. Without structured classification and protection policies, data remains vulnerable to breaches, insider threats, and compliance violations. Implementing a well-defined data classification framework helps organizations enforce appropriate security controls, regulatory compliance, and risk-based data handling practices.

Data classification is the process of categorizing information based on its sensitivity, value, and regulatory requirements. Organizations typically classify data into public, internal, confidential, and restricted categories, although classification levels may vary based on industry and business needs. Public data includes information that can be freely shared without risk, such as marketing materials and press releases. Internal data consists of business communications and operational documents intended for employees but not the general public. Confidential data includes proprietary business information, financial records, and strategic plans, requiring restricted access and encryption. Restricted data is the most sensitive, covering trade secrets, government-classified documents, and personal health records, requiring strict access controls, encryption, and compliance with industry regulations.

Regulatory compliance plays a significant role in defining data classification policies. Many industries must adhere to legal and regulatory frameworks such as GDPR, HIPAA, PCI DSS, SOX, and ISO 27001, which require organizations to protect sensitive data, enforce access controls, and implement security measures. For example, GDPR mandates strict handling of personal data, requiring organizations to classify, encrypt, and monitor access to ensure compliance with European privacy laws. HIPAA enforces rigorous safeguards on healthcare data, ensuring that medical records are protected against unauthorized access or disclosure. PCI DSS applies strict security standards to financial data, ensuring that credit card information is stored, processed, and transmitted securely.

Data discovery and classification tools help organizations automate data identification, tagging, and policy enforcement. These tools scan structured and unstructured data repositories, databases, cloud storage, and file systems to classify sensitive information based on predefined policies. Organizations leverage machine learning, artificial intelligence (AI), and pattern recognition algorithms to detect PII, financial data, intellectual property, and regulatory-protected data. Automated classification ensures that security teams maintain visibility over data flows, enforce compliance, and prevent data leaks.

Once data is classified, organizations implement data protection policies to enforce security measures that prevent unauthorized access, data loss, and exposure. Access control policies define who can access specific data, under what conditions, and with what level of privilege. Role-based access control (RBAC) and attribute-based access control (ABAC) ensure that employees, contractors, and third parties only access the data necessary for their job functions. Multi-factor authentication (MFA), least privilege access, and zero-trust security models further enhance access control policies, reducing insider threats and unauthorized data exposure.

Encryption is a critical component of data protection, ensuring that classified data remains secure during storage, transmission, and processing. Organizations implement AES-256 encryption for at-rest data, TLS encryption for data in transit, and homomorphic encryption for secure data processing. Cloud security policies require organizations to encrypt sensitive information stored in cloud environments, enforce key management best practices, and prevent unauthorized decryption. Regulatory frameworks such as GDPR and PCI DSS mandate encryption for sensitive data to mitigate the risk of data breaches.

Data loss prevention (DLP) solutions enforce data protection policies by monitoring, detecting, and blocking unauthorized data transfers. Organizations deploy network-based DLP, endpoint DLP, and cloud DLP to prevent data exfiltration, unauthorized sharing, and accidental leaks. DLP tools use content inspection, contextual analysis, and real-time monitoring to enforce security policies, ensuring that sensitive data remains within approved boundaries and compliance requirements.

Secure data retention and disposal policies ensure that sensitive information is stored securely and destroyed when no longer needed. Organizations define data retention schedules based on regulatory, legal, and business requirements, ensuring that records are kept only for the necessary duration. Secure disposal methods, including data shredding, cryptographic wiping, and degaussing, prevent data recovery from retired storage devices, hard drives, and cloud repositories. Regulations such as GDPR require organizations to delete personal data upon user request, enforcing data minimization and right-to-be-forgotten principles.

Insider threats pose a significant risk to data protection, requiring organizations to implement behavioral analytics, user activity monitoring, and anomaly detection to prevent data misuse. Employees, contractors, and privileged users may inadvertently or maliciously expose, alter, or steal sensitive data. Security teams enforce real-time access monitoring, privilege escalation detection, and automated alerts to detect suspicious data access patterns and mitigate risks. Implementing security awareness training programs ensures that employees understand their role in handling classified data responsibly.

Cloud security governance enforces data classification and protection policies across multi-cloud, hybrid cloud, and third-party service providers. Organizations define cloud security policies, enforce encryption standards, and monitor cloud storage access to prevent data breaches. Cloud access security brokers (CASBs) provide visibility into cloud data flows, detect unauthorized access, and enforce compliance with security policies. Organizations implement secure API integrations, identity federation, and cloud security posture management (CSPM) to maintain data integrity and regulatory compliance in cloud environments.

Incident response and data breach management are critical to mitigating the impact of security incidents involving classified data. Organizations develop incident response playbooks, forensic investigation protocols, and breach notification procedures to address data breaches efficiently. Regulatory laws such as GDPR require organizations to notify regulators and affected individuals within 72 hours of a data breach. Organizations implement real-time security analytics, automated threat detection, and cyber incident simulations to enhance data breach preparedness and compliance readiness.

Third-party risk management ensures that vendors, partners, and service providers comply with data classification and protection policies. Organizations conduct vendor security assessments, contractual security agreements, and continuous monitoring to enforce data protection standards across supply chain partners. Data protection addendums (DPAs) and compliance audits verify that third parties follow encryption policies, access control measures, and data retention guidelines. Security teams implement third-party risk scoring, security compliance validation, and automated vendor risk assessments to prevent supply chain vulnerabilities and regulatory violations.

Organizations integrate data classification and protection policies into cybersecurity frameworks, risk management programs, and compliance initiatives to safeguard sensitive information, prevent data breaches, and maintain regulatory adherence. Implementing automated classification tools, encryption best practices, DLP solutions, and strict access controls strengthens data security governance while minimizing exposure to cyber threats, insider risks, and compliance penalties. By defining clear policies, enforcing security controls, and fostering a security-conscious culture, organizations can effectively protect classified data and ensure long-term cybersecurity resilience.

Secure Cloud Governance and Compliance

Secure cloud governance and compliance are essential components of an organization's cybersecurity strategy, ensuring that cloud environments are managed securely, regulatory requirements are met, and data is protected against unauthorized access. As organizations increasingly adopt multi-cloud and hybrid cloud architectures, they face new challenges in access control, data protection, configuration management, and regulatory compliance. Cloud governance frameworks define security policies, risk management strategies, and operational controls to align cloud security with business objectives while maintaining compliance with GDPR, HIPAA, PCI DSS, ISO 27001, and other regulatory mandates.

Cloud governance establishes accountability, security policies, and oversight mechanisms to ensure that cloud services are deployed and managed securely. Organizations define cloud security policies that regulate access controls, encryption standards, data retention, and incident response procedures. Governance frameworks ensure that cloud security responsibilities are clearly assigned between internal IT teams, cloud service providers (CSPs), and third-party vendors. Organizations implement Cloud Security Posture Management (CSPM) solutions to continuously monitor cloud environments for misconfigurations, unauthorized changes, and compliance violations.

Regulatory compliance in cloud environments requires organizations to follow data protection laws, security standards, and industry-specific regulations. Many cloud compliance requirements mandate data encryption, audit logging, identity management, and access controls to protect sensitive data. Regulations such as GDPR enforce strict data privacy requirements, including data subject rights, breach notification obligations, and cross-border data transfer restrictions. HIPAA mandates security controls for cloud-based healthcare data, ensuring that electronic protected health information (ePHI) is encrypted, access-controlled, and audit-logged. PCI DSS compliance in the cloud requires organizations handling payment card data to follow encryption, network segmentation, and security monitoring best practices.

Cloud access control and identity governance ensure that only authorized users and devices can access cloud resources. Organizations implement Identity and Access Management (IAM), multi-factor authentication (MFA), and least privilege access to enforce strict security policies. Role-Based Access Control (RBAC) and Attribute-Based Access Control (ABAC) limit permissions based on user roles, job functions, and security attributes. Cloud-based Privileged Access Management (PAM) solutions monitor and secure administrative access to critical cloud services, preventing unauthorized privilege escalation and insider threats.

Data security in the cloud requires robust encryption, data loss prevention (DLP), and secure data sharing policies. Organizations enforce end-to-end encryption for data in transit and at rest to protect sensitive information from interception and unauthorized access. Cloud-native DLP solutions prevent unauthorized data transfers, monitor file-sharing activities, and enforce security policies to prevent data leaks. Tokenization and anonymization techniques enhance privacy by replacing sensitive data with masked or pseudonymized values, ensuring compliance with privacy regulations such as GDPR and CCPA.

Secure cloud configuration management ensures that cloud workloads, applications, and services are deployed following security best practices. Organizations implement Infrastructure as Code (IaC), automated compliance scanning, and security baselines to enforce consistent security configurations. Cloud Security Posture Management (CSPM) tools continuously assess cloud environments, detecting misconfigurations such as publicly exposed storage buckets, insecure API endpoints, and weak authentication settings. Security teams use policy-as-code frameworks such as Open Policy Agent

(OPA) and AWS Config Rules to automate compliance checks and enforce cloud security policies across multiple cloud providers.

Cloud monitoring and security analytics provide real-time visibility into cloud environments, detecting anomalous activities, unauthorized access, and potential security incidents. Organizations deploy cloud-native security solutions such as AWS Security Hub, Microsoft Defender for Cloud, and Google Security Command Center to aggregate security logs, analyze threat patterns, and detect compliance deviations. Security Information and Event Management (SIEM) integrations allow security teams to correlate cloud security events, detect suspicious behavior, and automate incident response workflows.

Third-party risk management in cloud environments ensures that vendors, cloud providers, and external partners follow security best practices. Organizations conduct third-party security assessments, vendor security audits, and compliance verification processes to assess the security posture of cloud providers. Shared responsibility models clarify security responsibilities between cloud customers and cloud providers, ensuring that security controls for identity management, encryption, and data governance are properly enforced. Organizations use vendor risk scoring, contractual security agreements, and continuous monitoring to reduce third-party risks.

Zero Trust security models enhance cloud governance by enforcing continuous verification, micro-segmentation, and adaptive security policies. Organizations implement Zero Trust Network Access (ZTNA) solutions to restrict access based on device security posture, user behavior, and contextual risk factors. Just-in-time (JIT) access models minimize the attack surface by granting temporary access to cloud resources only when needed. Zero Trust frameworks ensure that no cloud user, application, or device is implicitly trusted, reducing the risk of lateral movement and credential-based attacks.

Incident response and cloud forensics play a vital role in cloud governance and compliance. Organizations develop cloud-specific incident response plans, automated remediation workflows, and forensic investigation capabilities to detect and mitigate cloud security incidents. Security teams use cloud-native forensic tools, real-time security analytics, and AI-driven threat detection to investigate security breaches, unauthorized access attempts, and insider threats. Regulatory compliance mandates incident reporting timelines, breach notification procedures, and digital evidence retention policies, requiring organizations to document and analyze cloud security incidents thoroughly.

Cloud compliance automation streamlines governance by using AI-driven compliance tools, automated policy enforcement, and regulatory reporting dashboards. Organizations implement Cloud Compliance-as-Code (CaC) solutions to embed security policies into cloud development pipelines, ensuring that compliance requirements are met before workloads are deployed. Automated compliance assessments, cloud security audits, and real-time compliance dashboards help organizations maintain regulatory adherence while reducing manual audit efforts. Compliance automation improves security consistency, audit readiness, and governance transparency.

Secure cloud governance frameworks align cloud security strategies with business objectives, regulatory requirements, and risk management best practices. Organizations adopt governance frameworks such as NIST 800-53, ISO 27017 (Cloud Security Controls), and CSA Cloud Controls Matrix (CCM) to ensure that cloud security policies are enforced consistently across multi-cloud and hybrid cloud environments. Cloud governance policies define security ownership, cloud adoption strategies, and security performance metrics, ensuring that cloud risk management remains a top priority for security leadership and executive teams.

Organizations that implement strong cloud governance, compliance automation, and security best practices ensure cloud resilience, regulatory compliance, and data protection in increasingly complex cloud environments. Secure cloud governance frameworks provide visibility, accountability, and security enforcement mechanisms, enabling organizations to proactively manage cloud security risks, prevent compliance violations, and maintain trust in cloud-based services.

GRC Tools and Technology Solutions

Governance, Risk, and Compliance (GRC) tools and technology solutions play a critical role in helping organizations manage regulatory requirements, assess risks, and enforce security policies. As businesses operate in increasingly complex environments with evolving regulatory obligations, GRC platforms provide automation, real-time monitoring, and centralized risk management capabilities. These tools enable organizations to streamline compliance processes, enhance security posture, and integrate governance frameworks across IT and business functions.

GRC platforms offer risk assessment and management functionalities that help organizations identify, analyze, and mitigate potential threats. Advanced GRC tools use artificial intelligence (AI), machine learning, and predictive analytics to assess risks dynamically and provide real-time insights into vulnerabilities. Organizations leverage these tools to create risk heat maps, generate risk scores, and implement automated risk mitigation strategies. By integrating with security information and event management (SIEM) systems, intrusion detection systems (IDS), and endpoint protection platforms (EPPs), GRC solutions help security teams respond proactively to potential threats.

Regulatory compliance management is a core feature of modern GRC tools. Organizations must comply with GDPR, HIPAA, PCI DSS, SOX, ISO 27001, and other regulatory frameworks, requiring continuous tracking of security controls and legal obligations. GRC platforms provide automated compliance assessments, policy enforcement, and audit trail generation to ensure regulatory adherence. These tools offer compliance dashboards, automated gap analysis, and real-time alerts for non-compliance risks, reducing manual workload and enhancing transparency in regulatory reporting.

Policy management capabilities within GRC solutions allow organizations to define, distribute, and enforce security policies across departments and business units. GRC platforms support version control, policy lifecycle management, and automated policy updates to keep compliance requirements aligned with evolving regulations. By integrating with identity and access management (IAM) systems, GRC tools help organizations enforce role-based access control (RBAC), privileged access management (PAM), and multi-factor authentication (MFA) to ensure compliance with security policies.

Audit and reporting automation enhances the efficiency of internal audits, regulatory audits, and security assessments. GRC tools generate automated compliance reports, real-time security logs, and audit-ready documentation to support regulatory filings and security certifications. Organizations use these solutions to track audit findings, manage remediation tasks, and maintain evidence of regulatory compliance. Built-in AI-powered analytics, automated risk scoring, and compliance heat maps provide executives with insights into security trends and governance performance.

Third-party risk management is another essential feature of GRC platforms, enabling organizations to assess vendor security, monitor supply chain risks, and enforce contractual compliance. Organizations use GRC solutions to conduct third-party security audits, risk assessments, and continuous monitoring of vendor compliance. These tools integrate with cloud security posture management (CSPM), security rating platforms, and vendor risk scoring solutions to provide real-time visibility into external risks. Automated vendor risk questionnaires and third-party compliance tracking help organizations minimize exposure to supply chain vulnerabilities.

GRC technology solutions also include incident response and crisis management capabilities. Organizations use GRC platforms to develop incident response playbooks, automate security workflows, and coordinate response actions across teams. These tools integrate with security orchestration, automation, and response (SOAR) platforms, allowing organizations to automate threat containment, forensic investigations, and breach notification processes. By centralizing incident response documentation and post-incident reviews, GRC tools enhance cyber resilience and business continuity planning.

Fraud detection and financial compliance are enhanced through AI-driven anomaly detection, transaction monitoring, and anti-money laundering (AML) compliance. GRC tools integrate with fraud detection engines, financial security monitoring solutions, and real-time transaction risk analysis to identify suspicious activity.

Organizations use these tools to enforce regulatory compliance for financial transactions, detect insider threats, and prevent fraudulent activities. Machine learning models within GRC platforms continuously analyze transaction patterns to flag potential fraud risks before they escalate.

Cloud security and compliance automation are increasingly supported by GRC tools, ensuring that multi-cloud and hybrid cloud environments remain secure and compliant. Cloud-native GRC solutions integrate with cloud access security brokers (CASBs), cloud security posture management (CSPM) tools, and cloud governance frameworks to enforce real-time policy compliance, detect misconfigurations, and ensure regulatory adherence in cloud deployments. These solutions provide continuous compliance monitoring, cloud security analytics, and automated cloud security audits, reducing security gaps in cloud infrastructures.

Business continuity and disaster recovery planning are strengthened through GRC tools that enable organizations to assess business impact, create recovery plans, and automate crisis response scenarios. Organizations use GRC solutions to map critical business processes, identify dependencies, and ensure that disaster recovery measures align with compliance requirements. By integrating with cyber resilience frameworks, backup management systems, and incident response platforms, GRC tools help organizations maintain operational continuity during cyber incidents or regulatory disruptions.

Artificial intelligence and automation are transforming GRC technology by enhancing risk intelligence, compliance prediction, and threat analytics. AI-driven GRC solutions offer predictive risk modeling, natural language processing (NLP) for regulatory analysis, and automated compliance workflows. Organizations leverage AI to identify potential compliance violations, optimize security control configurations, and generate automated risk reports. AI-powered chatbots and virtual compliance assistants help security teams interpret regulatory updates, automate compliance checks, and provide real-time guidance on security policies.

GRC platforms are also integrating with blockchain technology to enhance regulatory transparency, audit integrity, and secure data governance. Blockchain-based GRC solutions provide immutable audit trails, smart contract compliance enforcement, and decentralized risk management frameworks. Organizations use blockchain to secure regulatory filings, prevent data tampering, and enable real-time compliance verification. These innovations improve trust, accountability, and efficiency in regulatory compliance management.

GRC technology solutions continue to evolve, offering advanced automation, real-time risk insights, and regulatory compliance capabilities to help organizations navigate complex cybersecurity and governance challenges. By leveraging cloud-native GRC platforms, AI-driven analytics, and blockchain-enabled security, organizations strengthen risk management, regulatory compliance, and security resilience in a rapidly changing digital environment.

Integrating GRC with DevSecOps

Integrating Governance, Risk, and Compliance (GRC) with DevSecOps is essential for ensuring that security, regulatory requirements, and risk management are embedded into software development processes. Traditional GRC frameworks often focus on manual compliance checks, periodic audits, and static risk assessments, while DevSecOps emphasizes automation, continuous security testing, and rapid development cycles. By aligning GRC with DevSecOps, organizations create a security-first culture where governance policies and compliance controls are integrated into the software development lifecycle (SDLC) without slowing down innovation.

GRC frameworks provide structured policies, regulatory guidelines, and risk management controls to enforce security best practices across IT environments. DevSecOps integrates security automation, continuous monitoring, and secure coding practices into development (Dev), security (Sec), and operations (Ops) workflows. Combining these methodologies ensures that security, risk, and compliance are addressed proactively and dynamically, reducing vulnerabilities and improving regulatory adherence throughout the development pipeline.

One of the key challenges in integrating GRC with DevSecOps is bridging the gap between security governance and agile software development. Traditional compliance audits often operate on fixed schedules and manual reviews, which do not align with DevSecOps principles of rapid releases, continuous integration, and automated testing. Organizations must transition from static compliance validation to continuous compliance monitoring by embedding automated security checks, policy-as-code frameworks, and real-time risk assessments into CI/CD pipelines.

Policy-as-code is a foundational approach for integrating GRC controls into DevSecOps. It enables organizations to codify security policies, compliance rules, and risk management requirements into machine-readable formats that can be automatically enforced. Tools such as Open Policy Agent (OPA), HashiCorp Sentinel, and AWS Config Rules allow teams to define and apply security governance policies across cloud configurations, application deployments, and infrastructure automation. By embedding compliance-as-code, organizations ensure that security and regulatory standards are continuously validated throughout the development lifecycle.

Automated security testing enhances GRC alignment with DevSecOps by ensuring that compliance violations, security misconfigurations, and code vulnerabilities are detected and remediated early in the SDLC. Organizations implement Static Application Security Testing (SAST), Dynamic Application Security Testing (DAST), and Software Composition Analysis (SCA) to scan code repositories, application runtime environments, and third-party dependencies for security weaknesses. Automated compliance scanners, such as Anchore, Checkov, and InSpec, validate security baselines against regulatory frameworks such as GDPR, PCI DSS, and NIST 800-53.

Risk management in DevSecOps requires real-time visibility into security threats, operational risks, and regulatory compliance gaps. Traditional GRC risk assessments often rely on manual reviews, periodic audits, and subjective risk scoring, which do not align with the continuous and iterative nature of DevSecOps. Organizations must adopt real-time risk monitoring tools, security analytics platforms, and AI-driven threat intelligence to dynamically assess security risks throughout the software development pipeline. Risk scoring models based on attack surface analysis, anomaly detection, and behavioral security analytics provide security teams with actionable insights into software vulnerabilities, configuration drift, and regulatory violations.

Compliance automation streamlines the enforcement of security policies, audit requirements, and regulatory mandates within DevSecOps workflows. Organizations implement continuous compliance validation tools that integrate with CI/CD pipelines to ensure that every code commit, infrastructure change, and deployment meets security and compliance standards. Cloud security posture management (CSPM) solutions, infrastructure-as-code (IaC) compliance scanners, and automated audit logging tools help organizations maintain compliance with industry regulations while accelerating development processes.

Identity and access management (IAM) governance is a critical component of integrating GRC with DevSecOps. Secure software development requires least privilege access, multi-factor authentication (MFA), and role-based access control (RBAC) to prevent unauthorized access to development environments, source code repositories, and production systems. Organizations enforce just-in-time (JIT) privileged access, zero-trust security models, and API access controls to mitigate the risk of insider threats, credential leaks, and unauthorized modifications to critical infrastructure.

Incident response and security monitoring capabilities must be integrated into DevSecOps pipelines to ensure that security events, policy violations, and compliance deviations are detected and remediated in real time. Organizations deploy Security Information and Event Management (SIEM) systems, Security Orchestration, Automation, and Response (SOAR) platforms, and real-time threat detection tools to monitor application logs, cloud security events, and network traffic anomalies. Automated security alerts, forensic logging, and compliance dashboards provide security teams with real-time insights into potential risks, misconfigurations, and regulatory non-compliance issues.

Third-party risk management is another key aspect of integrating GRC with DevSecOps. Organizations must ensure that open-source dependencies, containerized applications, and external APIs comply with security standards and licensing regulations. Software Bill of

Materials (SBOM) management, third-party risk scoring, and automated vulnerability scanning help organizations enforce security governance across third-party software components and supply chain dependencies. Tools such as Snyk, Trivy, and Black Duck automate the identification of third-party security vulnerabilities, outdated software packages, and compliance risks.

Secure cloud governance is essential for enforcing compliance, access controls, and security monitoring in cloud-based DevSecOps environments. Organizations implement cloud-native security frameworks, policy-based cloud security automation, and continuous compliance monitoring to ensure that cloud workloads meet regulatory standards. Cloud Security Posture Management (CSPM) solutions, Kubernetes security scanners, and serverless security monitoring tools help organizations enforce GRC controls within dynamic and scalable cloud infrastructures.

Training and security awareness programs play a crucial role in integrating GRC with DevSecOps. Development teams must be trained on secure coding best practices, compliance requirements, and risk management strategies to ensure that security is embedded throughout the SDLC. Organizations implement security champion programs, developer security training, and interactive threat modeling workshops to cultivate a security-first mindset among development and operations teams. Automated security coaching tools, such as GitHub Security Lab, CodeQL, and SonarQube, provide real-time feedback to developers on security vulnerabilities, compliance violations, and secure coding improvements.

Organizations that successfully integrate GRC with DevSecOps achieve continuous security validation, proactive risk management, and streamlined regulatory compliance without disrupting development velocity. By embedding policy-as-code, compliance automation, real-time security monitoring, and IAM governance into software development workflows, organizations create a scalable, secure, and compliance-driven DevSecOps ecosystem that aligns with industry best practices and regulatory requirements.

Measuring Cybersecurity Program Effectiveness

Measuring the effectiveness of a cybersecurity program is critical for ensuring that security investments align with organizational goals, mitigate risks, and comply with regulatory requirements. Organizations must continuously evaluate the performance of their security initiatives to identify weaknesses, improve defenses, and demonstrate accountability to stakeholders. A well-defined measurement framework provides quantifiable insights into security posture, risk exposure, and incident response capabilities, enabling organizations to make data-driven decisions and optimize their cybersecurity strategy.

Key performance indicators (KPIs) and key risk indicators (KRIs) serve as foundational metrics for assessing cybersecurity effectiveness. KPIs measure the performance of security controls, processes, and incident response, while KRIs identify emerging threats, vulnerabilities, and potential security risks. Common KPIs include mean time to detect (MTTD), mean time to respond (MTTR), security compliance rates, and phishing click-through rates. KRIs provide early warnings of security issues, such as unpatched vulnerabilities, unauthorized access attempts, and insider threat indicators. Organizations leverage automated security analytics platforms, SIEM solutions, and real-time dashboards to track these metrics and improve security decision-making.

Incident detection and response efficiency are key factors in evaluating cybersecurity effectiveness. Organizations must assess how quickly and accurately security teams can detect, analyze, contain, and remediate cyber threats. MTTD measures the average time required to detect a security incident, while MTTR quantifies how long it takes to respond and restore normal operations. A shorter MTTD and MTTR indicate a more effective security program, reducing the window of opportunity for attackers. Security operations centers (SOCs) use automated threat intelligence, AI-driven anomaly detection, and automated incident response playbooks to improve response times and reduce manual investigation workloads.

Vulnerability management metrics provide insights into how well organizations identify and mitigate security weaknesses. Metrics such as patching effectiveness, average time to remediate vulnerabilities, and percentage of critical vulnerabilities addressed within service-level agreements (SLAs) help organizations measure the efficiency of their threat and vulnerability management (TVM) programs. Organizations implement automated vulnerability scanners, penetration testing, and continuous security validation to ensure that vulnerabilities are identified and addressed before they can be exploited.

Security awareness and training effectiveness are crucial in preventing human-related security incidents. Organizations assess training programs by measuring phishing simulation success rates, security policy adherence, and the number of reported security incidents by employees. A decrease in phishing click rates and an increase in employee-reported security threats indicate an improved security culture. Security teams use interactive security training platforms, gamified awareness programs, and role-based security education to reinforce cybersecurity best practices among employees, executives, and third-party partners.

Compliance and regulatory adherence metrics evaluate whether an organization meets industry standards, legal requirements, and internal security policies. Compliance audit success rates, the number of non-compliance incidents, and regulatory breach penalties provide indicators of governance effectiveness. Organizations implement automated compliance monitoring, policy-as-code enforcement, and security control assessments to ensure adherence to frameworks such as GDPR, HIPAA, PCI DSS, and ISO 27001.

Endpoint and network security metrics assess the resilience of security controls in protecting devices, systems, and infrastructure. Organizations track malware detection rates, endpoint protection coverage, firewall rule violations, and unauthorized network access attempts to measure endpoint and perimeter defense effectiveness. Security teams deploy next-generation endpoint detection and response (EDR) solutions, zero-trust network segmentation, and intrusion prevention systems (IPS) to mitigate endpoint and network threats.

Threat intelligence integration plays a crucial role in measuring cybersecurity effectiveness by providing visibility into emerging cyber risks, attack campaigns, and adversary tactics. Organizations track threat intelligence accuracy, correlation success rates, and threat hunting effectiveness to evaluate how well security teams can predict, detect, and counteract cyber threats. Advanced threat intelligence platforms (TIPs) and AI-driven security analytics help automate threat correlation, detect unknown attack vectors, and enhance proactive threat hunting capabilities.

Cloud security effectiveness is assessed by measuring cloud misconfigurations, unauthorized access incidents, and compliance deviations in cloud environments. Organizations implement cloud security posture management (CSPM), cloud workload protection platforms (CWPP), and multi-cloud security analytics to monitor cloud security controls continuously. Metrics such as cloud access anomalies, API security violations, and compliance adherence in cloud deployments provide insights into cloud security governance and risk management effectiveness.

Identity and access management (IAM) metrics ensure that security teams can enforce strong authentication, least privilege access, and privileged account controls. Organizations track the number of failed login attempts, MFA adoption rates, privileged access violations, and identity governance policy enforcement to measure IAM effectiveness. Implementing risk-based authentication, just-in-time privileged access, and behavioral identity analytics enhances security visibility and reduces unauthorized access risks.

Cyber resilience and business continuity effectiveness are evaluated by measuring system downtime, recovery time objectives (RTO), recovery point objectives (RPO), and disaster recovery testing success rates. Organizations test incident response plans, cyber crisis simulations, and ransomware recovery strategies to ensure that business operations can recover quickly from cyber incidents, natural disasters, and security breaches. Security teams leverage automated backup validation, disaster recovery orchestration, and cyber resilience frameworks to enhance operational continuity.

Executive-level security metrics help communicate cybersecurity effectiveness to CISOs, board members, and business leaders. High-level security reports include risk exposure summaries, security investment ROI, and cyber risk mitigation effectiveness. Organizations use quantitative risk assessments, security heatmaps, and compliance scorecards to present security performance trends and align cybersecurity initiatives with business priorities.

Cybersecurity program effectiveness is continuously improved through benchmarking, security program maturity assessments, and continuous security validation. Organizations compare their security performance against industry peers, regulatory benchmarks, and historical data trends to identify areas for improvement. Security teams conduct gap analyses, cybersecurity audits, and red team exercises to validate security control effectiveness and refine risk management strategies.

By implementing a comprehensive cybersecurity measurement framework, organizations gain real-time visibility into security performance, identify risk trends, and ensure that security investments deliver measurable protection against cyber threats. Effective measurement practices enable proactive risk mitigation, continuous security optimization, and enhanced resilience against evolving cyber risks.

Red Team vs. Blue Team in Risk Governance

Red Team and Blue Team exercises play a crucial role in cybersecurity risk governance by testing an organization's security posture, identifying weaknesses, and improving defensive strategies. These simulations allow organizations to evaluate their ability to detect, respond to, and recover from cyber threats in real-world attack scenarios. The Red Team represents offensive security professionals who mimic real-world attackers, while the Blue Team consists of defenders responsible for detecting and mitigating attacks. By engaging in structured adversarial testing, organizations enhance their risk governance strategies, improve resilience, and strengthen their cybersecurity frameworks.

Red Team operations are designed to simulate real-world cyberattacks by employing the tactics, techniques, and procedures (TTPs) used by actual threat actors. These teams operate like ethical hackers or penetration testers, identifying exploitable vulnerabilities, security misconfigurations, and gaps in security policies. Red Team members utilize a wide range of attack techniques, including social engineering, phishing campaigns, privilege escalation, and lateral movement across networks. The goal is to test the effectiveness of an organization's security controls and identify weaknesses before malicious attackers can exploit them.

The Blue Team, on the other hand, is responsible for defending the organization's infrastructure, detecting threats, and responding to cyber incidents. Blue Team members include security analysts, incident responders, SOC operators, and IT administrators who continuously monitor for anomalies, unauthorized access attempts, and security breaches. Using tools such as Security Information and Event Management (SIEM) platforms, intrusion detection systems (IDS), endpoint detection and response (EDR) solutions, and threat intelligence feeds, the Blue Team works to detect, contain, and remediate cyber threats. Their primary goal is to minimize the impact of attacks, improve security monitoring, and refine incident response strategies.

Risk governance benefits significantly from Red Team vs. Blue Team simulations, as these exercises provide a realistic assessment of an organization's cybersecurity defenses. By exposing security gaps and testing response capabilities, organizations gain valuable insights into their risk exposure, defensive maturity, and areas for improvement. Red Team assessments help organizations identify high-risk attack vectors, misconfigurations, and weak access controls, while Blue Team responses provide data on detection efficiency, response times, and containment effectiveness.

One of the primary challenges in cybersecurity risk governance is identifying unknown vulnerabilities before attackers exploit them. Red Team operations uncover previously undetected weaknesses that could lead to data breaches, system compromises, or regulatory non-compliance. Blue Team defenders analyze these findings and implement security patches, enhanced monitoring, and risk mitigation measures to address vulnerabilities. Continuous Red Team vs. Blue Team engagements create a cyber-resilient environment where organizations proactively enhance their security posture.

Collaboration between Red and Blue Teams fosters a Purple Team approach, where both offensive and defensive teams work together to improve security strategies. The Purple Team model emphasizes knowledge sharing, real-time threat intelligence exchange, and collaborative security enhancement. Red Team members provide insights into attacker methodologies, advanced persistent threats (APTs), and social engineering tactics, while Blue Team members refine their detection algorithms, security logging, and forensic analysis capabilities. This iterative feedback loop strengthens risk governance by continuously adapting security defenses based on real-world attack simulations.

Regulatory compliance frameworks, such as NIST 800-53, ISO 27001, GDPR, PCI DSS, and HIPAA, require organizations to conduct regular security assessments, vulnerability testing, and incident response drills. Red Team assessments contribute to compliance validation by identifying compliance gaps, security misconfigurations, and policy violations. Blue Team documentation of security incidents, response effectiveness, and mitigation measures ensures audit readiness and regulatory adherence. Risk governance integrates Red Team exercises into compliance reporting, security control validation, and board-level risk assessments to maintain a robust security program.

Threat intelligence plays a crucial role in Red Team vs. Blue Team engagements by enhancing adversary simulation, improving threat detection, and refining defensive strategies. Red Teams use threat intelligence feeds, dark web monitoring, and attack surface analysis to simulate the latest cyber threats accurately. Blue Teams leverage real-time threat indicators, automated security alerts, and behavioral analytics to detect and respond to evolving attack techniques. Organizations that incorporate threat intelligence-driven adversarial testing strengthen their cyber resilience and risk management strategies.

Incident response planning benefits from Red Team vs. Blue Team exercises by validating response workflows, testing security playbooks, and improving organizational preparedness. Red Team attacks simulate real-world cyber incidents, such as ransomware infections, insider threats, and supply chain attacks, challenging Blue Team defenders to execute effective response strategies. These simulations help organizations refine their incident containment procedures, forensic investigation processes, and disaster recovery plans. By stress-testing incident response capabilities, organizations ensure that security teams can quickly contain and remediate cyber incidents while minimizing operational disruptions.

Cybersecurity risk governance relies on continuous risk assessment, proactive threat mitigation, and adaptive security frameworks. Red Team vs. Blue Team engagements contribute to ongoing security validation, executive-level risk reporting, and board-level cybersecurity decision-making. Organizations that integrate continuous adversarial testing into their governance models maintain proactive risk mitigation, improve security investments, and align cybersecurity initiatives with business objectives.

Red Team vs. Blue Team testing strengthens cybersecurity risk governance by providing real-world attack simulations, improving security defenses, and ensuring compliance with regulatory requirements. By leveraging collaborative security models, continuous security assessments, and automated threat intelligence, organizations enhance their ability to detect, respond to, and mitigate cyber threats before they cause significant damage.

Managing Insider Threats in GRC

Managing insider threats is a critical component of Governance, Risk, and Compliance (GRC), as insider risks pose a significant challenge to organizational security. Unlike external cyber threats, insider threats originate from individuals within the organization, such as employees, contractors, vendors, or business partners. These individuals have legitimate access to sensitive systems, data, and resources, making insider threats difficult to detect and mitigate. A robust GRC framework integrates policy enforcement, risk management, security controls, and continuous monitoring to reduce the likelihood of insider threats and ensure compliance with regulatory requirements.

Insider threats can be malicious or unintentional. Malicious insiders deliberately misuse their access to steal sensitive information, commit fraud, sabotage systems, or assist external attackers. These threats may be motivated by financial gain, revenge, espionage, or ideological reasons. Unintentional insider threats, on the other hand, stem from human error, negligence, or lack of security awareness, leading to data breaches, accidental data sharing, or misconfigurations that expose critical systems. Both types of threats require proactive risk governance, security awareness training, and behavioral monitoring to mitigate risks effectively.

GRC frameworks establish insider threat policies, access control mechanisms, and compliance enforcement to safeguard sensitive information. Organizations define acceptable use policies (AUPs), role-based access control (RBAC), and least privilege access models to limit exposure to critical data. Governance frameworks, such as ISO 27001, NIST 800-53, and CIS Controls, mandate strict identity and access management (IAM) policies to prevent unauthorized privilege escalation. By enforcing zero-trust security models and continuous authentication, organizations minimize the risk of insider-driven security incidents.

Risk management in insider threat programs involves identifying high-risk users, analyzing behavioral anomalies, and implementing security controls. Organizations deploy user and entity behavior analytics (UEBA) to monitor login patterns, file access activities, email communications, and data transfer behaviors. Advanced security analytics detect deviation from normal behavior, unauthorized data exfiltration attempts, and privilege abuse. Risk-based security policies flag high-risk users, enforce security controls, and trigger automated incident response workflows to contain potential insider threats before they escalate.

Access control and privileged account monitoring are key elements of insider threat prevention in GRC. Organizations implement privileged access management (PAM) solutions to restrict administrative access and enforce just-in-time (JIT) privilege escalation. Strong authentication measures, such as multi-factor authentication (MFA) and biometric verification, reduce the risk of compromised credentials. Security teams conduct periodic access reviews, privilege audits, and session monitoring to ensure that high-risk activities are logged, analyzed, and reported.

Data loss prevention (DLP) solutions enforce real-time data security policies, block unauthorized file transfers, and prevent insider-driven data leaks. Organizations deploy endpoint DLP, network DLP, and cloud DLP to monitor and restrict email attachments, file uploads, and data movement across organizational boundaries. Enforcing data encryption, secure file-sharing policies, and access logging ensures that classified information is protected against insider threats. Compliance frameworks, such as GDPR, HIPAA, and PCI DSS, require organizations to enforce strict data handling policies and maintain audit trails for sensitive data access.

Behavioral risk scoring enhances insider threat detection and response by assigning risk levels to employees based on security behaviors, role sensitivity, and access history. Security teams analyze unusual data access trends, off-hour login attempts, and excessive privilege requests to identify potential threats. AI-driven predictive analytics models detect insider threats in real time, enabling automated security enforcement and proactive risk mitigation.

Incident response and forensic investigation are critical for managing insider threat incidents. Organizations establish incident response playbooks, forensic analysis procedures, and breach notification protocols to contain and investigate insider attacks. Security teams use digital forensics tools, log correlation techniques, and forensic data reconstruction to identify compromised accounts, analyze attack patterns, and gather evidence for legal and compliance reporting. Regular red team vs. blue team exercises test insider threat detection capabilities and response effectiveness.

Security awareness training and cultural reinforcement reduce unintentional insider threats by educating employees on phishing awareness, password hygiene, and data security best practices. Organizations implement role-based security training, phishing simulation exercises, and insider threat awareness campaigns to ensure that employees recognize and report suspicious activities. Encouraging a security-conscious culture, anonymous reporting mechanisms, and ethical security practices enhances organizational resilience against insider risks.

Vendor and third-party risk management ensures that external entities with privileged access to internal systems follow security best practices. Organizations enforce third-party security audits, contractual data protection agreements, and continuous monitoring to prevent insider threats originating from contractors, consultants, or outsourced IT teams. Security teams use vendor risk scoring, supply chain security monitoring, and access governance policies to mitigate risks posed by third-party insiders.

Regulatory compliance frameworks enforce strict insider threat mitigation measures to ensure organizations maintain legal accountability, security governance, and risk mitigation. SOX (Sarbanes-Oxley Act), NIST Cybersecurity Framework, and ISO 27035 (Incident Management) require organizations to log access activities, enforce least privilege principles, and implement risk-based security controls. Compliance audits evaluate insider risk exposure, security policy adherence, and regulatory reporting accuracy. Organizations use GRC automation tools to maintain compliance records, generate audit reports, and demonstrate regulatory adherence.

Monitoring and continuous security validation are essential for proactively managing insider threats. Organizations deploy security orchestration, automation, and response (SOAR) solutions to detect, analyze, and respond to insider threats in real time. Automated security incident correlation, threat intelligence enrichment, and real-time security dashboards provide security teams with a comprehensive view of insider risk trends.

Managing insider threats within a GRC framework requires policy-driven security governance, real-time risk detection, and continuous monitoring. By integrating behavioral analytics, identity governance, data loss prevention, and security awareness training, organizations enhance their ability to detect, mitigate, and prevent insider-driven security incidents while maintaining compliance with regulatory mandates.

National and International Cybersecurity Regulations

Cybersecurity regulations at both national and international levels are essential for ensuring the protection of sensitive data, securing critical infrastructure, and enforcing accountability in digital environments. Governments and regulatory bodies worldwide have established cybersecurity laws, data protection frameworks, and industry-specific compliance requirements to mitigate cyber risks and promote secure digital ecosystems. These regulations define the legal and operational standards that organizations must follow to safeguard information systems, prevent cyber threats, and ensure privacy rights.

National cybersecurity regulations vary across jurisdictions, reflecting regional security priorities, legal traditions, and technological advancements. In the United States, multiple regulatory frameworks govern cybersecurity across different sectors. The Cybersecurity Information Sharing Act (CISA) encourages organizations to share cyber threat intelligence with the government, while the Health Insurance Portability and Accountability Act (HIPAA) mandates stringent security controls for healthcare data. The Gramm-Leach-Bliley Act (GLBA) enforces cybersecurity standards for financial institutions, and the Federal Information Security Modernization Act (FISMA) establishes security requirements for federal agencies. The U.S. Securities and Exchange Commission (SEC) has also introduced cybersecurity disclosure rules, requiring publicly traded companies to report material cybersecurity incidents and risk management strategies.

The European Union (EU) has implemented some of the most comprehensive cybersecurity regulations, with the General Data Protection Regulation (GDPR) serving as a global benchmark for data privacy and security. GDPR mandates strict data protection measures, transparency in data processing, and hefty penalties for non-compliance. It grants individuals the right to access, correct, and delete their personal data, while requiring organizations to implement encryption, risk assessments, and breach notification procedures. The EU also enforces the Network and Information Security Directive (NIS2), which sets cybersecurity standards for critical infrastructure operators and digital service providers, requiring them to enhance cyber resilience, conduct risk assessments, and establish incident response mechanisms.

In China, cybersecurity is tightly regulated under the Cybersecurity Law (CSL), the Data Security Law (DSL), and the Personal Information Protection Law (PIPL). These regulations impose strict data localization requirements, cross-border data transfer restrictions, and compliance obligations for foreign companies operating in China. The Multi-Level Protection Scheme (MLPS) categorizes information systems based on their security level and mandates compliance with strict security controls, network monitoring, and government audits. Organizations handling sensitive data, critical infrastructure, or cloud services in China must comply with extensive security verification and approval processes.

The Asia-Pacific region has also seen significant cybersecurity regulatory developments. Japan's Act on the Protection of Personal Information (APPI) enforces data protection and breach notification requirements, aligning closely with GDPR principles. Singapore's Cybersecurity Act mandates that critical information infrastructure (CII) operators implement security measures and report cybersecurity incidents. Australia's Security of Critical Infrastructure Act (SOCI) requires operators in sectors such as energy, telecommunications, and banking to comply with cybersecurity risk management obligations.

In Latin America, cybersecurity regulations are evolving as governments recognize the increasing risks of cyberattacks. Brazil's General Data Protection Law (LGPD) establishes data protection rights, security obligations, and penalties for non-compliance, similar to GDPR. Mexico's Federal Law on Protection of Personal Data Held by Private Parties governs data privacy and cybersecurity compliance for businesses. Other Latin American countries, including Argentina, Chile, and Colombia, have implemented cybersecurity frameworks, incident reporting laws, and financial sector regulations to strengthen digital security.

Cybersecurity regulations for financial institutions are particularly stringent due to the high risk of fraud, data breaches, and cyber-enabled financial crimes. The Payment Card Industry Data Security

Standard (PCI DSS) applies globally to organizations handling credit card transactions, requiring strict encryption, access controls, and network security measures. The Bank for International Settlements (BIS) and Financial Stability Board (FSB) set international cybersecurity guidelines for the financial sector, including cyber risk assessments, fraud detection strategies, and digital identity security controls. The Basel Committee on Banking Supervision (BCBS) enforces cybersecurity risk management policies to protect global financial systems from cyber threats.

Cybersecurity regulations also extend to critical infrastructure protection, ensuring that essential services such as power grids, water treatment plants, transportation systems, and healthcare networks remain secure. The U.S. Cybersecurity and Infrastructure Security Agency (CISA) enforces security measures for critical infrastructure operators, while the EU's NIS2 Directive mandates cyber resilience and risk mitigation strategies for essential service providers. Canada, the United Kingdom, and Australia have implemented similar cybersecurity mandates to safeguard critical infrastructure from cyberattacks.

Cloud security compliance is another growing regulatory concern, with governments enforcing strict security requirements for cloud service providers (CSPs), data centers, and SaaS platforms. The Federal Risk and Authorization Management Program (FedRAMP) in the U.S. sets security standards for cloud services used by government agencies. The EU's proposed Cybersecurity Certification Scheme for Cloud Services (EUCS) aims to establish uniform security certification requirements for cloud providers operating in Europe. The ISO/IEC 27017 and ISO/IEC 27018 standards provide global best practices for securing cloud environments and protecting personally identifiable information (PII) in cloud computing.

Artificial intelligence (AI) and emerging technologies are now subject to cybersecurity regulations as governments address AI-driven cyber threats, algorithmic bias, and automated security decision-making. The EU AI Act proposes a risk-based regulatory framework that classifies AI applications based on their security and ethical impact, imposing strict compliance requirements for high-risk AI systems. The U.S. National Institute of Standards and Technology (NIST) AI Risk

Management Framework provides guidelines for ensuring AI transparency, security, and accountability. As AI and machine learning become integral to cybersecurity operations, organizations must comply with evolving AI security governance laws and ethical AI guidelines.

International cybersecurity cooperation has become a priority for global regulatory bodies as cyber threats increasingly transcend national borders. The Budapest Convention on Cybercrime, led by the Council of Europe, establishes international cooperation mechanisms for cybercrime investigation, law enforcement collaboration, and evidence sharing. The United Nations (UN) Open-ended Working Group on Cybersecurity promotes global cyber stability through international norms, capacity-building initiatives, and cyber diplomacy agreements. Countries participate in cyber threat intelligence sharing alliances, such as the Five Eyes (U.S., UK, Canada, Australia, New Zealand), the European Union Agency for Cybersecurity (ENISA), and the ASEAN Cybersecurity Cooperation Strategy, to enhance global cyber resilience.

Cybersecurity regulations will continue to evolve as governments address rising cyber threats, digital sovereignty concerns, and the expansion of cloud, AI, and IoT security risks. Organizations must proactively monitor regulatory changes, implement compliance automation, and integrate security governance frameworks to ensure adherence to both national and international cybersecurity laws. By aligning corporate security policies with regulatory requirements, adopting risk-based compliance approaches, and participating in global cybersecurity cooperation, organizations can strengthen their cyber resilience and regulatory readiness.

Cybersecurity Budgeting and Investment Strategies

Cybersecurity budgeting and investment strategies are essential for organizations to effectively allocate resources, mitigate risks, and strengthen their overall security posture. As cyber threats evolve, businesses must adopt risk-based financial planning to ensure that security investments align with their most critical vulnerabilities and compliance obligations. A well-structured cybersecurity budget balances preventive measures, detection capabilities, incident response, and regulatory compliance, ensuring that security spending maximizes protection while optimizing operational costs.

A risk-based approach to cybersecurity budgeting prioritizes security investments based on threat landscapes, industry-specific risks, and business impact assessments. Organizations conduct cyber risk assessments, penetration testing, and attack surface analysis to identify the most high-risk assets, potential attack vectors, and security gaps. Cybersecurity budgets should focus on addressing high-impact threats, protecting mission-critical systems, and ensuring compliance with regulatory frameworks such as GDPR, HIPAA, PCI DSS, and NIST 800-53.

Security budgeting must account for direct and indirect costs associated with cybersecurity initiatives. Direct costs include hardware, software, security personnel, and third-party security services, while indirect costs encompass incident recovery expenses, regulatory fines, reputational damage, and lost business opportunities resulting from cyber incidents. Organizations use cyber risk quantification models, financial impact analysis, and cost-benefit assessments to justify security investments and demonstrate return on security investment (ROSI) to executive leadership.

Cybersecurity investments are often categorized into foundational, operational, and strategic expenses. Foundational investments include firewalls, intrusion detection systems (IDS), endpoint security solutions, and encryption technologies that form the core security infrastructure. Operational expenses cover security operations center (SOC) staffing, incident response teams, continuous security monitoring, and third-party risk management programs. Strategic investments focus on emerging security technologies, artificial intelligence-driven threat detection, zero-trust security architectures, and cloud security frameworks that enhance long-term cybersecurity resilience.

Balancing proactive and reactive security spending ensures that organizations invest in preventative controls while maintaining adequate incident response capabilities. Preventative investments include employee security awareness training, secure software development practices, and vulnerability management programs. Reactive investments focus on incident detection, forensic investigation, breach remediation, and disaster recovery planning. A well-balanced cybersecurity budget allocates funding to both threat prevention and incident response, reducing the financial and operational impact of cyberattacks.

Cybersecurity budgeting also considers third-party security services and managed security providers (MSPs). Organizations increasingly rely on outsourced SOC operations, managed detection and response (MDR), and cloud security services to supplement internal security capabilities. Security-as-a-Service (SECaaS) models offer cost-effective, scalable security solutions, allowing organizations to optimize security spending, reduce operational overhead, and access advanced security expertise without the high costs of maintaining in-house teams.

Security automation and artificial intelligence (AI) play a critical role in optimizing cybersecurity budgets by reducing manual security tasks, improving threat detection efficiency, and enhancing response automation. Organizations invest in security orchestration, automation, and response (SOAR) platforms, AI-driven SIEM solutions, and automated compliance monitoring to streamline security operations and reduce reliance on costly manual security workflows. AI-driven cybersecurity investments improve threat detection accuracy, reduce mean time to detect (MTTD) and mean time to respond (MTTR), and enhance overall risk governance.

Cloud security budgeting requires a dedicated financial strategy to address the security challenges of multi-cloud and hybrid cloud environments. Organizations allocate funds for cloud security posture management (CSPM), cloud access security brokers (CASB), and cloud workload protection platforms (CWPP) to ensure continuous monitoring and policy enforcement in cloud ecosystems. Security teams implement policy-based cloud security budgeting, automated cloud compliance assessments, and cloud-native security controls to maintain regulatory compliance and minimize cloud security risks.

Regulatory compliance and legal obligations significantly influence cybersecurity investment strategies. Non-compliance with data protection laws, financial security regulations, and industry-specific cybersecurity mandates can result in financial penalties, legal disputes, and operational disruptions. Organizations allocate funds for compliance automation tools, security audits, governance frameworks, and legal advisory services to ensure adherence to evolving regulatory requirements. Proactive compliance spending reduces the risk of regulatory fines, litigation costs, and reputational damage.

Board-level cybersecurity budgeting discussions focus on aligning security investments with business objectives, enterprise risk management (ERM), and digital transformation initiatives. Executives evaluate security budget justifications, cyber risk tolerance levels, and security program maturity assessments to determine optimal spending levels. Security leaders present quantifiable security performance metrics, risk mitigation outcomes, and compliance readiness reports to justify cybersecurity expenditures and secure executive buy-in for security initiatives.

Cyber insurance is an increasingly important component of cybersecurity investment strategies. Organizations assess cyber insurance policies, coverage limits, and risk transfer options to mitigate financial losses from data breaches, ransomware attacks, and business interruptions. Cyber insurance complements security investments by covering incident response costs, legal expenses, regulatory fines, and data recovery expenses. However, insurers may require organizations to meet minimum security standards and risk assessment requirements before issuing coverage.

Measuring the effectiveness of cybersecurity spending involves tracking key performance indicators (KPIs) and key risk indicators (KRIs) to evaluate security program efficiency. Organizations analyze incident detection rates, vulnerability remediation timelines, compliance audit success rates, and phishing awareness improvements to assess whether security investments yield tangible risk reduction and operational benefits. Cybersecurity benchmarking against industry peers, regulatory standards, and historical security performance trends helps organizations refine their budgeting strategies.

Future cybersecurity investments must account for emerging threats, evolving attack techniques, and next-generation security technologies. Organizations allocate research and development (R&D) budgets for quantum-resistant encryption, AI-driven threat prediction, blockchain-based security models, and zero-trust network architectures. Long-term security investment planning ensures that organizations stay ahead of cyber adversaries, regulatory changes, and digital transformation risks.

A well-structured cybersecurity budget ensures that organizations achieve proactive risk mitigation, regulatory compliance, and operational security resilience. By integrating risk-based financial planning, strategic security investments, and continuous security program evaluations, organizations optimize cybersecurity spending while maximizing threat prevention, incident response, and business continuity capabilities.

Emerging Technologies and Cyber Risk Management

Emerging technologies are transforming the cybersecurity landscape, introducing both new opportunities and risks. As organizations adopt artificial intelligence (AI), machine learning (ML), cloud computing, blockchain, quantum computing, and the Internet of Things (IoT), they must integrate advanced cyber risk management strategies to mitigate evolving threats. While these technologies enhance automation, operational efficiency, and security capabilities, they also create new attack vectors, regulatory challenges, and cyber resilience concerns. A proactive cyber risk management approach ensures that security frameworks evolve alongside technological advancements, reducing the likelihood of cyber incidents, regulatory violations, and operational disruptions.

Artificial intelligence and machine learning play a significant role in threat detection, security automation, and predictive risk analytics. AI-driven cybersecurity solutions analyze large datasets, detect patterns in cyber threats, and automate security response workflows. Machine learning enhances behavioral threat detection, anomaly identification, and adaptive security controls, reducing false positives and improving response times. However, AI also introduces risks such as adversarial AI attacks, algorithmic biases, and data poisoning threats, where attackers manipulate AI models to bypass security controls. Organizations must implement AI security governance, model validation techniques, and adversarial defense strategies to ensure AI-driven cybersecurity remains secure, transparent, and resilient.

Cloud computing has revolutionized IT infrastructure, enabling scalable, on-demand computing resources and distributed security models. However, the shift to multi-cloud and hybrid cloud environments introduces risks such as misconfigurations, insecure API integrations, data breaches, and identity compromise. Organizations implement Cloud Security Posture Management (CSPM), Cloud Access Security Brokers (CASB), and Zero Trust Network Access (ZTNA) to enforce security policies, monitor access control, and prevent data leaks. Cloud risk management requires continuous security monitoring, automated compliance assessments, and cloud-native security frameworks to mitigate threats and ensure regulatory adherence.

Blockchain technology enhances data integrity, secure transactions, and decentralized authentication mechanisms, reducing fraud risks and unauthorized data alterations. Blockchain's immutable ledger technology provides enhanced auditability, supply chain security, and secure identity management. However, cyber risks associated with blockchain include smart contract vulnerabilities, cryptographic key theft, and decentralized financial (DeFi) security breaches. Organizations deploying blockchain solutions must implement secure coding practices, smart contract auditing, and cryptographic key governance to mitigate risks while leveraging blockchain's security benefits.

Quantum computing represents both a breakthrough and a cybersecurity challenge. Quantum computing's ability to process complex calculations at unprecedented speeds threatens traditional encryption algorithms, including RSA and ECC, which are widely used for secure communications, financial transactions, and authentication mechanisms. Organizations must prepare for post-quantum cryptography (PQC) adoption, quantum-safe encryption algorithms, and quantum-resistant cybersecurity frameworks to mitigate future quantum-related security risks. Governments and industry leaders invest in quantum encryption, quantum key distribution (QKD), and cryptographic agility to ensure long-term data security resilience.

The Internet of Things (IoT) introduces new cyber risks due to the massive scale of interconnected devices, weak security configurations, and supply chain vulnerabilities. IoT devices, ranging from industrial sensors to consumer smart appliances, often lack firmware updates, strong authentication, and network segmentation, making them attractive targets for botnet attacks, ransomware infections, and distributed denial-of-service (DDoS) attacks. Organizations deploy IoT security frameworks, network access control (NAC), and endpoint security monitoring to reduce attack surfaces and enforce device authentication, data encryption, and firmware integrity verification.

5G networks accelerate high-speed data connectivity, real-time communication, and low-latency applications, driving advancements in autonomous vehicles, smart cities, and industrial automation. However, 5G cybersecurity challenges include increased attack surfaces, unsecured network slicing, and potential vulnerabilities in software-defined networking (SDN). Security strategies for 5G risk management focus on zero-trust architectures, secure 5G infrastructure design, and continuous threat monitoring. Organizations collaborate with telecommunication providers, government agencies, and security researchers to enhance 5G security standards, regulatory compliance, and secure network operations.

Zero Trust security models provide a robust risk management framework for emerging technologies by enforcing continuous authentication, least privilege access, and micro-segmentation. As organizations integrate AI, cloud computing, IoT, and 5G, Zero Trust principles ensure that no user, device, or application is implicitly trusted, reducing the risk of insider threats, supply chain attacks, and credential compromises. Implementing risk-based authentication (RBA), software-defined perimeter (SDP) security, and just-in-time (JIT) access provisioning strengthens cybersecurity governance in modern digital ecosystems.

Cyber risk quantification enables organizations to measure, prioritize, and mitigate risks associated with emerging technologies. Advanced cyber risk analytics, financial impact modeling, and attack surface visualization help security teams assess the likelihood and consequences of cyber threats. Organizations implement risk-based cybersecurity budgeting, continuous security validation, and automated risk reporting dashboards to optimize security investments while minimizing operational disruptions, data breaches, and regulatory fines.

Cyber insurance plays an increasing role in risk management for organizations adopting emerging technologies. Insurers assess AI-driven fraud risks, cloud security posture, quantum computing threats, and IoT device vulnerabilities before issuing cyber risk coverage. Organizations must meet minimum security requirements, conduct cyber risk assessments, and implement proactive security controls to qualify for cyber insurance policies covering incident response, ransomware recovery, and legal liabilities. Cyber risk governance frameworks integrate cyber insurance planning, risk transfer strategies, and regulatory compliance validation to enhance overall cyber resilience.

Cybersecurity regulatory compliance frameworks continue evolving to address emerging technology risks. Governments and regulatory bodies enforce AI security standards, cloud security certifications, IoT device security mandates, and quantum-resistant encryption policies to mitigate future cyber risks. Organizations align cybersecurity programs with NIST AI Risk Management Framework, GDPR AI compliance guidelines, ISO 27017 cloud security controls, and national cybersecurity regulations to ensure adherence to evolving security requirements.

Cyber threat intelligence (CTI) enhances real-time risk visibility, emerging threat analysis, and proactive defense strategies for emerging technologies. Organizations integrate AI-driven threat detection, cloud-based cyber intelligence sharing, and IoT security telemetry analytics to anticipate and mitigate advanced persistent threats (APTs), zero-day exploits, and AI-powered cyberattacks. Cyber risk management platforms leverage automated threat correlation, deep learning-driven attack prediction, and adversarial AI defenses to strengthen cyber resilience.

Managing cyber risks in emerging technologies requires a multi-layered security strategy, continuous threat monitoring, and proactive security governance. Organizations adopt AI-powered security automation, cloud-native security frameworks, blockchain-based identity management, and post-quantum encryption strategies to safeguard digital assets and maintain regulatory compliance. Advanced cyber risk management ensures that businesses leverage innovation while mitigating evolving cybersecurity threats in an increasingly interconnected world.

Cybersecurity Maturity Models and Assessments

Cybersecurity maturity models and assessments provide organizations with structured methodologies to evaluate, improve, and optimize their security posture. These models help organizations identify strengths, weaknesses, and gaps in their cybersecurity programs, enabling them to develop risk-based strategies for continuous security improvement, regulatory compliance, and threat mitigation. Maturity assessments guide security teams in aligning policies, processes, and technical controls with industry best practices and evolving cyber threats.

A cybersecurity maturity model establishes progressive security capability levels, allowing organizations to benchmark their security posture, measure operational effectiveness, and track improvements over time. Maturity levels typically range from basic security awareness and reactive defenses to advanced, adaptive, and predictive cybersecurity strategies. Organizations use maturity models to determine where they stand in their cyber resilience journey and define clear objectives for security enhancement.

The NIST Cybersecurity Framework (NIST CSF) is one of the most widely used maturity models, providing a structured approach for managing cybersecurity risk. It consists of five core functions: Identify, Protect, Detect, Respond, and Recover, which help organizations build comprehensive security programs. The NIST CSF maturity levels range from Partial (informal security measures) to Adaptive (fully integrated risk-driven security practices). Organizations conduct NIST CSF assessments to evaluate their risk management capabilities, implement security controls, and enhance cyber resilience.

The Cybersecurity Capability Maturity Model (C2M2), developed by the U.S. Department of Energy, focuses on critical infrastructure cybersecurity assessments. It provides a structured approach for organizations to assess security program maturity across domains such as risk management, situational awareness, and incident response. The C2M2 framework defines maturity levels from Initiating to Optimized, guiding organizations in progressively improving their security controls and governance structures.

The Capability Maturity Model Integration (CMMI) for Cybersecurity is another widely used assessment model that evaluates security governance, risk management, and operational security controls. CMMI defines maturity levels from Initial (ad hoc processes) to Optimized (fully integrated, risk-driven cybersecurity operations). Organizations leverage CMMI assessments to develop structured security improvement roadmaps, align cybersecurity with business objectives, and measure compliance with regulatory frameworks.

The ISO 27001 Maturity Model provides a structured approach for organizations to assess information security management system (ISMS) effectiveness. ISO 27001 assessments focus on risk management, security governance, and regulatory compliance. Organizations evaluate their security control implementation, risk mitigation effectiveness, and continuous improvement processes based on ISO 27001 maturity levels. Achieving a higher ISO 27001 maturity level ensures that organizations maintain a proactive, well-documented, and resilient security framework.

Cybersecurity maturity assessments rely on quantitative and qualitative evaluation methods to measure security effectiveness. Organizations use risk assessment questionnaires, security control audits, threat modeling, and penetration testing to gather actionable insights into security program performance. Maturity assessments provide detailed reports, risk scoring, and compliance gap analyses, enabling security teams to prioritize remediation efforts, technology investments, and policy enhancements.

Security program benchmarking is a key component of cybersecurity maturity assessments. Organizations compare their security maturity scores against industry benchmarks, regulatory standards, and peer organizations to evaluate their standing in cybersecurity best practices and compliance readiness. Benchmarking enables data-driven decision-making, investment prioritization, and continuous security enhancement.

A cybersecurity maturity roadmap defines short-term, mid-term, and long-term security improvement initiatives based on assessment findings. Security teams develop structured action plans, technology adoption strategies, and security awareness programs to progress toward higher maturity levels. Organizations implement automated security frameworks, AI-driven threat detection, and security policy automation to advance their cybersecurity maturity.

Governance, Risk, and Compliance (GRC) platforms integrate cybersecurity maturity models into security governance, risk management, and audit workflows. Organizations use GRC tools to automate security assessments, track risk mitigation progress, and generate compliance reports. Integrating cybersecurity maturity models with GRC solutions enhances security oversight, regulatory compliance monitoring, and executive-level security reporting.

Continuous cybersecurity improvement requires regular maturity assessments, security gap analyses, and adaptive risk management strategies. Organizations conduct annual security audits, automated security posture assessments, and red team/blue team exercises to validate security effectiveness, incident response capabilities, and threat mitigation readiness. Advanced cybersecurity maturity models leverage machine learning, cyber risk analytics, and security automation to enhance real-time risk management.

Cybersecurity maturity models and assessments help organizations achieve proactive risk management, regulatory compliance, and operational security resilience. By implementing structured evaluation frameworks, automated risk assessment tools, and continuous security optimization strategies, organizations strengthen their defense capabilities against evolving cyber threats while ensuring business continuity and regulatory alignment.

Future Trends in Cybersecurity GRC

The future of Governance, Risk, and Compliance (GRC) in cybersecurity is evolving rapidly as organizations face increasingly sophisticated cyber threats, regulatory changes, and digital transformation challenges. Emerging trends in GRC focus on automation, artificial intelligence (AI), regulatory harmonization, risk quantification, and continuous compliance monitoring. As cyber risks become more dynamic, organizations must adopt adaptive security frameworks, zero-trust architectures, and AI-driven risk management solutions to enhance their security posture and regulatory compliance.

AI and machine learning are transforming cybersecurity GRC by automating risk assessments, compliance reporting, and security decision-making. AI-driven GRC platforms analyze threat intelligence feeds, security logs, and regulatory changes to provide real-time risk insights and automated compliance validation. Machine learning models detect anomalous user behavior, emerging cyber threats, and policy violations, enabling security teams to prioritize risk mitigation efforts and enforce adaptive security controls. AI-powered security analytics enhance incident response, forensic investigations, and compliance audits, reducing manual workload and improving security efficiency.

Regulatory harmonization is becoming a priority as organizations struggle to comply with multiple cybersecurity frameworks and data protection laws. Governments and regulatory bodies are working toward global cybersecurity standards and cross-border compliance alignment. The adoption of common cybersecurity frameworks, such as ISO 27001, NIST 800-53, and the EU NIS2 Directive, simplifies compliance processes and enhances security governance. Future cybersecurity GRC strategies will integrate automated compliance tracking, AI-driven regulatory intelligence, and policy-as-code enforcement to ensure seamless regulatory adherence across multiple jurisdictions.

Cyber risk quantification is gaining traction as organizations seek data-driven approaches to assess cybersecurity investments and risk exposure. Traditional qualitative risk assessments are being replaced by quantitative cyber risk models that calculate financial impacts, threat likelihoods, and security control effectiveness. Organizations leverage cyber risk scoring systems, attack surface visualization, and financial risk modeling tools to translate cybersecurity risks into business-relevant financial metrics. This approach enables security leaders to prioritize cybersecurity investments, justify security budgets, and optimize risk mitigation strategies.

Zero-trust security models are becoming the foundation of cybersecurity GRC frameworks. As cyber threats evolve, organizations are shifting from perimeter-based security to identity-driven, least-privilege access models. Zero-trust architectures enforce continuous authentication, micro-segmentation, and contextual security policies to prevent unauthorized access. Future GRC strategies will integrate zero-trust policy automation, risk-adaptive access controls, and AI-driven identity verification to strengthen governance, risk, and compliance in modern IT environments.

Cloud-native security governance is critical as organizations migrate to multi-cloud and hybrid cloud infrastructures. Traditional compliance models designed for on-premises security do not scale to dynamic cloud environments. Future GRC frameworks will emphasize cloud security posture management (CSPM), continuous cloud compliance monitoring, and cloud access security brokers (CASBs) to enforce real-time security policies and automated risk mitigation. Organizations will implement serverless security models, workload protection strategies, and API security governance to address emerging cloud threats.

Blockchain technology is being integrated into cybersecurity GRC to enhance data integrity, regulatory transparency, and tamper-proof audit logs. Blockchain-based GRC solutions enable immutable security records, decentralized identity management, and automated regulatory compliance tracking. Smart contracts enforce real-time policy compliance, risk scoring automation, and secure third-party transaction verification. As blockchain adoption increases, organizations will leverage decentralized cybersecurity frameworks, tokenized access controls, and blockchain-powered threat intelligence sharing to enhance risk governance.

Cybersecurity resilience frameworks are evolving to incorporate adaptive risk management, automated threat response, and predictive security analytics. Organizations are adopting cyber resilience maturity models that integrate security, business continuity, and crisis management into a unified GRC strategy. Future cybersecurity resilience frameworks will include AI-driven security orchestration, autonomous risk response mechanisms, and real-time cyber crisis simulations to prepare organizations for rapid threat adaptation and regulatory compliance continuity.

Third-party risk management is becoming increasingly critical as organizations expand their reliance on external vendors, cloud service providers, and software supply chains. Future GRC strategies will integrate continuous vendor security monitoring, automated third-party risk scoring, and AI-driven supply chain security analytics. Organizations will implement real-time risk validation, blockchain-powered vendor compliance tracking, and automated contract security enforcement to reduce supply chain vulnerabilities and regulatory exposure.

Cybersecurity automation and compliance-as-code (CaC) are revolutionizing GRC efficiency and regulatory enforcement. Organizations are moving away from manual security audits and compliance documentation to automated security policy validation, AI-driven compliance enforcement, and real-time regulatory reporting. Compliance-as-code integrates security governance policies directly into development pipelines, cloud environments, and infrastructure-as-code (IaC) deployments, ensuring continuous regulatory adherence. Future GRC frameworks will adopt automated security control verification, AI-driven policy audits, and real-time risk dashboards to streamline compliance management.

Cyber insurance markets are evolving to accommodate dynamic cyber risks, ransomware threats, and regulatory fines. Future cybersecurity GRC strategies will integrate cyber risk transfer models, AI-powered cyber insurance underwriting, and automated breach impact assessments to optimize cyber insurance policies, risk mitigation strategies, and financial recovery planning. Organizations will leverage real-time security posture assessments, cyber risk scoring models, and automated policy compliance validation to reduce cyber insurance premiums and enhance financial protection against cyber incidents.

Behavioral analytics and insider threat management are becoming key focus areas for cybersecurity GRC. Organizations will deploy AI-driven insider risk analytics, real-time user behavior monitoring, and continuous security awareness training to detect insider anomalies, privilege abuse, and policy violations. Future GRC strategies will integrate automated insider threat detection, role-based risk assessments, and AI-powered employee risk profiling to strengthen security governance and mitigate internal security risks.

Cyber threat intelligence (CTI) is playing an increasingly proactive role in cybersecurity risk management and compliance enforcement. Future GRC models will incorporate AI-driven cyber threat intelligence, automated attack prediction, and real-time risk scoring mechanisms to anticipate and prevent cyber threats before they escalate. Organizations will leverage automated threat hunting, adversary simulation models, and AI-powered security analytics to ensure continuous risk mitigation and compliance adaptation.

Cybersecurity governance, risk, and compliance will continue to evolve through automation, AI-driven decision-making, zero-trust adoption, and cloud-native security frameworks. Organizations must embrace continuous compliance monitoring, AI-powered risk assessments, and automated policy enforcement to stay ahead of emerging threats, regulatory changes, and digital transformation challenges. By adopting advanced GRC technologies, risk-based security frameworks, and proactive cyber resilience strategies, organizations will enhance their security posture, regulatory readiness, and operational cybersecurity efficiency in the future cybersecurity landscape.

Conclusion and Final Recommendations

Cybersecurity Governance, Risk, and Compliance (GRC) are foundational pillars in managing modern cyber risks, ensuring regulatory adherence, and maintaining organizational resilience. As cyber threats continue to evolve, organizations must adopt proactive, risk-based security strategies, automated compliance frameworks, and continuous threat monitoring to stay ahead of attackers. Effective GRC programs integrate security governance, risk quantification, compliance automation, and adaptive defense mechanisms to mitigate cyber risks while aligning with business objectives. Organizations that prioritize cybersecurity GRC strengthen their ability to detect, respond to, and recover from cyber incidents while minimizing financial, operational, and reputational damage.

A comprehensive cybersecurity governance framework defines security policies, accountability structures, and risk management processes to ensure that security efforts align with organizational priorities. Executive leadership, security teams, and compliance officers must collaborate to establish clear cybersecurity roles, risk ownership models, and board-level security oversight. Governance frameworks such as NIST Cybersecurity Framework (CSF), ISO 27001, and CIS Controls provide structured approaches for developing cybersecurity policies, risk assessment methodologies, and incident response playbooks. Organizations must adopt a top-down cybersecurity governance model where security is integrated into corporate risk management, IT governance, and regulatory compliance initiatives.

Risk management in cybersecurity requires continuous assessment, real-time risk quantification, and dynamic threat modeling to identify and mitigate security vulnerabilities. Organizations must implement cyber risk management frameworks, attack surface analysis, and threat intelligence-driven security controls to prevent data breaches, ransomware attacks, insider threats, and supply chain vulnerabilities. Cyber risk assessment models should incorporate quantitative risk scoring, financial impact simulations, and AI-driven risk analytics to ensure that security investments align with the most critical risks. By integrating zero-trust security architectures, predictive risk modeling, and behavioral threat detection, organizations can enhance cyber resilience and operational security readiness.

Regulatory compliance is a critical component of cybersecurity GRC, ensuring that organizations meet legal, industry-specific, and international security requirements. Compliance mandates such as GDPR, HIPAA, PCI DSS, NIS2, and SOX require organizations to enforce strict data protection policies, implement encryption controls, and maintain incident reporting readiness. Organizations should invest in compliance automation tools, security policy-as-code solutions, and AI-driven regulatory intelligence to streamline compliance workflows and reduce the complexity of managing multiple cybersecurity regulations. Regular security audits, penetration testing, and continuous compliance monitoring improve regulatory adherence while strengthening overall cybersecurity posture.

Automation and artificial intelligence (AI) play a key role in enhancing cybersecurity GRC by reducing manual security tasks, improving threat detection accuracy, and enforcing real-time compliance validation. Organizations must leverage AI-driven security analytics, automated risk assessment tools, and machine learning-powered anomaly detection systems to predict, prevent, and respond to cyber threats efficiently. Security orchestration, automation, and response (SOAR) platforms enhance incident response speed, automate threat hunting processes, and improve security workflow efficiency. Organizations should integrate AI-powered security solutions into SIEM, endpoint protection, and identity governance frameworks to optimize cybersecurity operations.

Zero-trust security principles must be embedded into cybersecurity governance to enforce continuous authentication, least-privilege access control, and micro-segmentation. Traditional perimeter-based security models are no longer effective in modern cloud, hybrid, and remote work environments. Organizations should implement identity and access management (IAM) solutions, risk-based authentication mechanisms, and continuous security validation techniques to eliminate implicit trust and enforce strict security verification across all users, devices, and applications. By adopting zero-trust architectures and just-in-time (JIT) access provisioning, organizations can significantly reduce the risk of credential compromise, insider threats, and unauthorized access.

Cloud security governance is essential as organizations continue migrating workloads, applications, and sensitive data to multi-cloud and hybrid cloud environments. Cloud security strategies must incorporate cloud-native security frameworks, cloud security posture management (CSPM), and secure API governance policies to enforce security compliance, prevent data breaches, and mitigate cloud misconfigurations. Organizations should implement continuous security monitoring, automated cloud security controls, and secure software development lifecycle (SSDLC) policies to protect cloud workloads, containerized applications, and serverless computing environments.

Cybersecurity training and awareness programs are fundamental to reducing human-related security risks, including phishing attacks, credential theft, and unintentional data exposure. Organizations should develop ongoing security training programs, simulated cyberattack exercises, and interactive security awareness initiatives to improve employee vigilance, security culture, and policy adherence. By incorporating role-based cybersecurity training, social engineering prevention techniques, and real-time security awareness tools, organizations can reduce security incidents caused by human error while improving overall cyber hygiene.

Third-party risk management is a growing cybersecurity concern as organizations rely on external vendors, cloud service providers, and software supply chain integrations. Security teams must conduct vendor security assessments, implement contractual security requirements, and continuously monitor third-party risk exposure to prevent supply chain vulnerabilities. Automated third-party risk scoring, blockchain-based compliance verification, and continuous vendor security audits help organizations enforce strong security standards across external business relationships. Establishing zero-trust third-party access controls and continuous security monitoring for vendor interactions minimizes supply chain attack risks and regulatory liabilities.

Cyber insurance is becoming an important component of cyber risk mitigation strategies, covering financial losses related to data breaches, ransomware attacks, and legal liabilities. Organizations should assess cyber insurance policies, incident response coverage, and financial risk transfer strategies to protect against monetary damages from cybersecurity incidents. Cyber insurance providers now require robust security controls, threat mitigation measures, and real-time security posture assessments to determine insurance coverage eligibility and premium rates. Organizations should integrate cyber risk quantification models and automated risk reporting tools to optimize cyber insurance planning and financial risk mitigation.

Cyber resilience and business continuity planning must be integrated into cybersecurity governance to prepare for, respond to, and recover from cyber incidents. Organizations should develop incident response playbooks, disaster recovery protocols, and cyber crisis simulation exercises to strengthen their ability to maintain operations during cyberattacks, natural disasters, and IT disruptions. Security teams must implement real-time backup validation, ransomware recovery strategies, and automated failover systems to ensure that critical business functions remain resilient against cyber threats.

Future cybersecurity GRC strategies will emphasize continuous compliance validation, AI-driven risk intelligence, and automated cybersecurity governance frameworks. Organizations must adopt proactive risk management, real-time security policy enforcement, and adaptive threat response models to protect against evolving cyber risks and regulatory challenges. By integrating advanced security automation, zero-trust architectures, and predictive cybersecurity analytics, organizations can enhance their security resilience, regulatory compliance, and operational risk management capabilities in an increasingly complex cybersecurity landscape.